DOMESTIC DETENTION

RODNEY PEMBERTON

13TH & JOAN

DOMESTIC DETENTION. Copyright 2023 by Rodney Pemberton. All rights reserved. No part of this publication may be reproduced, distributed, or transmitted in any form or by any means, including photocopying, recording, or other electronic or mechanical methods, without the prior written permission of the publisher, except in the case of brief quotations embodied in critical reviews and certain other noncommercial uses permitted by copyright law.

For permission requests, write to the publisher, addressed "Attention: Permissions Coordinator," 205 N. Michigan Avenue, Suite #810, Chicago, IL 60601. 13th & Joan books may be purchased for educational, business or sales promotional use. For information, please email the Sales Department at sales@13thandjoan.com.

Printed in the U. S. A.

First Printing, November 2023

Library of Congress Cataloging-in-Publication Data has been applied for.

ISBN: 978-1-953156-93-8

ACKNOWLEDGMENTS

To my relatives and their spouses on both sides, thank you. This book would not exist without you, especially those on my mother's side. Without you, my journey would have been impossible. My biggest regret is knowing that my aunt, who recently passed, will never get the opportunity to read this book. Knowing how much she was always there for my mother and everyone else is something that I can never thank her for enough.

To my older sister: Be strong and keep pushing. It's not over yet.

Kay-Kay, Bapsy, and Princess: I'm your brother, not your cousin.

My neighbors and friends in St. Vincent: Thank you for the fun growing up. It was what helped to take my mind off everything that was happening, especially Desiree (Ingrid Quammie). Thank you for your decades of friendship.

Jomo Thomas: Great job and my hat's off to you.

Sofia Phillips: Words can't express your friendship and honesty for the decades we've known each other. Thanks for your support through it all.

Debra Brizan: Wow! It's like I've known you forever. You were the first friend I had when I got here, and it's safe to say that you're a never-ending friend. Thank you very much.

Nadeen Neil: You thought I'd forget you, ha. Nope! Not for one minute. Thank you very much for listening.

Verne Smith: How many years can I count? Wow! You may no longer be a New Yorker, lol, but the friendship continues.

Jennifer Doughty: Thank you. It was very interesting the way we met and to this day, I still thank Dillon.

Kim (Petra Pope), we haven't seen each other in decades, but: Thank you.

Sophia Johnson: Thank you and Yulla. Please forgive me for not remembering your last name, but thanks for your listening ear.

Stella Eyewumi: How can I ever forget you? We've lost contact for almost two decades, and I can't seem to find you on social media, but thank you for listening. I pray that you'll come across this book, see my Instagram at the back of it, and contact me.

Sandra Harrison: Thank you. The year was 2004, which seems like yesterday, but how time flies.

Gyllian, Geoffrey, Ralph Defaria: Thank you all.

George Bellamy: Thank you for the cod fish and dumplings you brought me each morning after you saw that I was losing a lot of weight, and to the wonderful staff at Cooper Robertson and Partners who welcomed me onboard, and treated me as part of the family. Thank you, and you wondered why I stayed so long? lol.

FX Collaborative: Thank you for the time, it was greatly appreciated. Tim, Stefhan Cavezzeali, Peter Ogman Jason Voss, Teyana, Patty Wong, Jamal, Ashley, Amina, Phil, Ram, Adriana Calle, Jeff, Toby Snyder, Carol Hsiung, Henry Pemberton, and the rest of the staff whose names I may not remember, thank you for making me feel welcome.

Bluedge: Thank you for the years. It was a long journey, but nothing lasts forever.

To my "Islandmix," " Go Jamaica, " and "Radio Jamaica" family, thanks for your laughter. It was something that I needed at the time, especially those of you who I pulled over to my Facebook. Thank you. Woot! woot! Big up to you, Yeah man!

To the staff at 13th and Joan: Thank you so much for your patience, especially Kath, Candace, and Rasheda. The artwork is amazing. The journey wasn't easy, but with dedication, we did it, and thank you very much.

To my younger sister: You're a true champion and a hero without a cape. Your dedication at four years of age to our mother is all the proof needed to show how much you loved her. Although we were all robbed of her physical love, one thing no one could ever take from her was her generosity toward everyone, and to me, wow! The only thing I can say is thank you God because without you, I couldn't have made it this far. Yes, the mental pain lingers and the tears flow at times, especially when I had to relive everything while writing this manuscript, but my mental pain is enough to show everyone that I am never easily broken. No book is big enough to document everything, but the 10% revealed is enough to bring me comfort. Everything else will remain discreet.

THANKS TO THE CREATOR!

CONTENTS

Chapter One: The Journey Begins 3

Chapter Two: Under Suspicion 13

Chapter Three: The Absence 36

Chapter Four: Clues to a Missing Trail 45

Chapter Five: The Arrangement 62

Chapter Six: The Mission 73

Chapter Seven: The Reunion 84

Chapter Eight: Facing the Ordeal 141

Chapter Nine: The Challenge 156

Chapter Ten: The Deceiver 165

Chapter Eleven: The American Dream 180

Chapter Twelve: Welcome Home 212

Chapter Thirteen: Farewell 219

Chapter Fourteen: Karma and the Conclusion 225

INTRODUCTION

THE BOND BETWEEN A MOTHER AND SON IS UNIQUE AND CANNOT be broken. So years after my mother migrated and married, I knew that something was wrong when the birthday and Christmas cards she always sent to my sister and I came to a sudden halt. Calls that she made frequently decreased to about once every two months and only came at a time when her husband was away from home. A tremble that indicated a panicked woman pleading for a way out was noticeable in her voice. Family members who reached out to her caused her number to either change each time or disconnected as she moved from state to state into unfamiliar suburbs thousands of miles away from New York City where she was only surrounded by his family. Handwritten letters began to appear at least six to eight months apart, all scribbled as if they were written by a three-year-old before she suddenly went missing. Several attempts were made by mail to contact her, but all were stamped "Return to sender." Many began to assume that she was dead, but I was convinced that she needed to be rescued from a husband who had an obsession for control over a quiet woman who refrained from altercations, which made her susceptible to him. Being her only son meant that it was my responsibility to find her. I first cried out to God and kept my plan a secret out of concern that disclosing any information would have given many the impression that I was a madman searching for a woman whose whereabouts were unknown.

On a sunny Monday afternoon, I left the Caribbean Island of St. Vincent and the Grenadines with two photographs of her along with all of her last known addresses and made my way to New York City with the intention of reaching out to the FBI but instead, a few phone calls led to a state over a thousand miles away. She was found confined to a wheelchair, paralyzed from below her waist, with her torso trembling constantly like a woman with Parkinson's in a house with her four-year-old daughter and a barbaric husband who never informed anyone in her family about her condition, even though he had our addresses and telephone numbers.

CHAPTER ONE:
THE JOURNEY BEGINS

It was Mom's final hours at the airport as I watched her slim figure from 10 feet away, standing at the check-in counter. She was dressed in a beige pantsuit with diamond stud earrings and her natural hair length extended onto the back of her shoulders. Suspecting that she wasn't returning anytime soon, I secretly made my way over to the waving gallery and was instantly intrigued by the handful of small aircraft parked on the tarmac. I was completely mesmerized for about 15 minutes as my imagination took me on a journey where I began to picture myself piloting one of the aircraft. Suddenly, I felt the palm of her hand resting on my shoulder and turned to see her towering over me. As our eyes met, I looked toward the ground without even saying a word. There was complete silence for a moment before she finally asked: "Do you want something to eat?" "No," I replied, even though I was hungry. My lack of appetite somehow satisfied my hunger and caused me to turn my full attention back onto the aircraft. To avoid breaking my concentration, she walked away and joined my grandfather, aunt, and my sister who were all quietly dining at a table just feet away.

For about an hour and a half, I quietly stood in isolation, making sure that I was still in their sight, quietly glancing at the mountainous terrain from time to time until my eyes met a shiny dot distance away as if it was hovering in mid-air. I watched it transform into a tiny aircraft that grew enormously before descending onto the runway, producing puffs of smoke that spewed from each tire as they hit the tarmac. The aircraft then slowly approached the terminal with a deafening sound, and my heart began to pound faster against my chest. I knew it was only a few minutes before my mother stepped onto that aircraft without me knowing when I would see her again.

I turned to see her approaching me with her eyelids drooping and a facial expression of a smirk that conveyed a potent message of someone with a broken heart. Without saying a word, she squatted before me and looked me in the eyes for a moment. I felt a sensation of dejection that left me at the brink of tears, then beneath my breath asked, "When are you coming back?" Instead of responding, she placed her arms around me for a moment before gently kissing me on the forehead. As I looked at her, the tears in her eyes confirmed all my suspicion that she wasn't returning anytime soon. Without saying a word, she released me from the hug, then approached my sister who was standing only feet away and said something to her before kissing her on the cheeks. We watched her walk toward the departure room, stop one final time inside the doorway and stare at us before swiping her fingers below her eyes to remove the tears from her cheeks. My heart stopped and I quietly inhaled, then released just loud enough to hear myself as she smirked one final time before disappearing inside the departure room, leaving the door to slowly close behind her.

"She's gone," I said to myself as my aunt, sister, grandfather, and I made our way toward the waving gallery. As much as I tried my best to quietly stand with my back turned toward the aircraft out of fear that seeing her ascending the stairway would cause me to tear up, a touch on my shoulder from the palm of my aunt's hand caused me to turn. Just as I did, I saw my mother climbing the stairwell of the aircraft. My eyes became watery as she waved one final time.

Fifteen minutes later we were home. As everyone exited the car and made their way inside the house, I remained seated outside on a rock, carved just a few feet away from the entrance of the house. Staring blankly at the ground, I reminisced on all of the trips she took on her vacation leave from a nearby island where she was employed. For the rest of the day, I secluded myself inside a bedroom where my uncle slept. It wasn't until we received a call from her that night that I exited the room. The first question she asked was "How are you doing?" "Fine," I responded, knowing very well that I wasn't. I couldn't restrain myself from asking, "When are you coming back?" At that moment, there was complete silence on the phone before I began to hear her sob. It made me feel guilty enough that I decided that it was time to pass the phone over to my sister.

I raced back inside my uncle's room and quietly sat on the bed with my eyes staring blankly through the closed glass window in complete silence. It was where I remained for most of the time, rarely having contact with the outside world except for during church services, school, or whenever the loud barking of my neighbor's German shepherd drew me toward the fence. Many thought that he was wild but to me, he was only protecting his master's territory. After noticing how hairy he was, I wanted to pet him. One day I couldn't resist and approached the fence and saw him sitting peacefully outside his cage with his back turned toward me. As much as I was tempted to leap the fence and comb his furry hair with the palm of my hands, I still didn't trust him and decided to peer over the fence instead. In the blink of an eye, he sensed my presence, then turned and looked at me as if I was a possible intruder. As our eyes met, his ears raised but I didn't panic. "Hey, Teddy boy," I said, and he sighed, then moaned. "Come here, Teddy boy, come here," I continued, thinking that a friendship was developing between us. Instead, he growled, and stared at me with an intimidating look then without warning, launched at me, only to be stopped by the lengthy rope around his neck. I darted away from the fence and raced through the street until I got to a quiet street where one of my uncles and a few school friends were engaged in a game of cricket.

One of the boys saw me approaching and straight away shouted "Ah, look, the man who called himself Abdul Qadir," one of the world's greatest spin bowlers from a very long time ago. Another boy shouted, "Give him the ball. Let's see what he can do." "I'm sure he's all full of mouth," another said. Hearing them jeering me put me under tremendous pressure, and I needed to prove to them that I wasn't any coward. "Well, gimme the ball, and I'll show you," I said boasting, and was handed the ball right away. As the eruption of jeers continued, the batsman nervously took the wicket. Like a professional spin bowler, I stepped back, ran forward, swung my hand, then released the ball and watched as it moved toward the batsman who kept his eyes on it and then with perfect timing, swung his bat with such an extreme force that the only thing everyone heard was a tap produced from the ball hitting the bat. The ball hit the bulb on the street pole and shattered it into shards of glass that hit the ground, and splashed into splinters before it vanished. Everyone sucked their teeth with their heads shaking in disappointment as they looked toward me. Some busted out laughing in enjoyment, then the heckling began. "Man, go and look for the ball," one man burst out. Another shouted, "Man, you bowled the ball so slowly that everyone had enough time to read all the letters written on the ball." Another burst out, "You should be playing netball with the girls instead of playing cricket with us." A brawl unexpectedly broke out and the loud use of profanity was heard by neighbors, including a woman who was a member of a church where many of my relatives attended.

Without even identifying the person who used the profanity, the lady quickly informed my grandfather who, within minutes, came barging toward us with a rope over his shoulder. His lips were bitten and his facial expression indicated anger. My uncle looked at me, wondering if we should both take off running but for some reason, he decided to remain seated on a wall built by a few workers who were constructing a nearby building. To this day, I'm not sure if his reason for not running was due to the heckling he would have probably received the following day or if he thought that my grandfather was bluffing. Without saying a word, my grandfather swung the rope with extreme force across my uncle's back. I watched in shock with my eyes widened as dust spewed off his T-shirt like a puff of Sahara dust. It sent my uncle taking off like a rocket before disappearing around a corner. Someone shouted "Boy, run," but I figured that there wasn't any need to since no one inside the house had ever laid a hand on me. As he looked at me, his demeanor changed. He was probably shocked enough to see me still standing there. There wasn't even a smirk on his face as he stared at me. As panic set in, I tried to take off, but my knees somehow buckled and prevented me from moving. My grandfather bit his lip for a second time, then swung the rope that connected directly into the center of my back. I felt a sharp, burning sensation quiver down my back that caused me to wiggle like a snake. I screamed out a note much higher than a female opera singer, then took off like an Olympian sprinter reacting to a starting pistol. I leaped a six-foot fence that I couldn't clear under normal circumstances, landed on both feet into a woman's backyard, then outran her three dogs. To this day, I am still convinced that the speed at which I took off running after that blow was a lot quicker than Usain Bolt's 9.58, 100 meters, and the height in which I cleared the fence was nothing less than a world record that will never be broken.

The next day at school the heckling began and I decided that it was best to remain isolated, and ignored everyone until someone pushed me into a classmate who was standing mischievously inside the doorway to prevent me from entering. "Excuse me," I said, and he replied, "Move me," with a mischievous grin on his face. To avoid any fight, I calmly walked toward a second door, but he had already gotten there before me, standing inside the doorway with both arms extended across both sides. "Excuse me," I said for a second time, and he burst out laughing. I shook my head and was about to walk away when suddenly, someone pushed me from behind with such force that it sent me flying violently into him, knocking him off his feet and onto the ground. I wasted no time in leaping back onto my feet in search of the perpetrator and made the mistake of leaving my back turned toward the boy who fell to the ground. From behind, I felt a knuckle connect directly to my left eye that instantly caused me to see stars twirl and twinkle. Every possible color flashed before my eyes along with identifying images that I couldn't describe. Out of fear that I had lost vision, I held my eye and crouched to the ground in pain, then was continuously punched and kicked over my entire body. The continuous squealing of "Wee," and "Fight, fight," rang out by bystanders but I was too scared to defend myself out of fear that removing my hands from over my eyes would only expose my other eye to a second punch. Finally, the kicking and the punching stopped and someone brought me onto my feet. "Are you ok?" they asked. As the muffling sound of boos continued from the small crowd and with one eye closed and my fists folded, I flew into the air with extreme rage like a Kung Fu master, and launched at my attacker with the intention of kicking him into his chest, then punched him back into his eyes, but was instantly grabbed and restrained by an adult who picked me up with one hand and dangled me like a flag hanging from a pole. The news reached my grandfather in no time, and I was forbidden from hanging out with anyone except for the boys around the area who I normally played cricket with at the nearby park.

Everything was happening so fast and since it was the end of the school term, I was curious as to how I was about to cope with being at home every day all because of an unfortunate situation that I never instigated. Just as school vacation began, a relative introduced my uncle and me to a herd of rabbits and guinea pigs that I wasn't too fond of. The rabbits were ok but the guinea pigs somehow reminded me of giant rats, and I didn't want to have any part of it. Plus, finding them food was new to us since we were just two city boys with absolutely no knowledge of animals except for dogs and cats. We were informed by a friend that their main source of food was vines so we began to make round trips of up to two kilometers to fields with trenches of potato plants. Out of ignorance, we plowed them all by hand and stuffed them into crocus bags, not knowing that each time we were innocently causing the farmer to lose hundreds or even possibly thousands of dollars. Weeks after innocently dwindling the poor people's field without them reaping any crops or profits, I became an altar boy at the nearby Anglican Church where my grandfather on my father's side was an organist.

As the vacation continued, there wasn't much to do except prepare for high school. There were a few for me to choose from but after some pondering, the Intermediate High School, AKA "Timmy," was chosen due to its unusual school hours of 8:15 a.m. to 1:15 p.m. that coincided with my aunt's working schedule. I can still remember that Friday afternoon of enrollment. The sky was cloudless and the sun was brilliant but brutal. At exactly 1 p.m., my aunt knocked on the door that was situated just behind the back of the school on a quiet street. "Come in," the faint husky voice of the headmaster yelled out. I looked at my aunt who smiled at me as I shrugged my shoulders, then smiled back at her. She turned the door handle and made her way in as I followed right behind, and there he was, reclined in his chair with both feet extended on his desk. He was staring into a newspaper from behind a pair of glasses just resting on the tip of his nose and hanging by a string attached around his neck. "Sit down," he said. As much as I tried to hold the laugh in, I found myself chuckling. My aunt pulled a chair and sat, then I quietly sat beside her with my eyes glued on him as I was intrigued by his mannerism. It must have been about a minute or two of silence as he continued to read his newspaper before he finally said "Lemme see what you have." I giggled again as my aunt reached into her bag and handed him the documents. With his full attention still on the newspaper article, he extended his hand as my aunt placed the documents into his palm. It was as if he was so caught up in whatever he was reading that he couldn't afford to lose focus. I continued to chuckle, which was very much uncontrollable, but my aunt kept her laughter in. Suddenly, "What's your name?" he asked. My aunt quickly answered, which finally got his attention as he looked away from the newspaper for the first time to peer at my aunt and me from beneath the lens of his glasses. He slowly put the newspaper away and began to scrutinize the documents. Many would consider his mannerisms to be eccentric but for me, they were unique and something that I had never experienced before. Deep inside, I was very much determined to figure him out.

Finally, for the first time, he removed the glasses from the bridge of his nose, stared at my aunt, then asked a few more questions which she answered without hesitation. It was as if he couldn't wait to respond and yell "Accepted," like an excited kid in the back of a classroom eager to answer a question. My aunt looked at me and smiled, then I watched him get to his feet and saw that he wasn't as tall as I had imagined. What grabbed my attention was his attire. All the men I knew around his age, including both my grandfathers, wore their shirts tucked inside their pants that were pulled almost up to their chest with a tightly secured belt and the buckle turned to one side. The headmaster's style was the complete opposite. His sparkling clean, white shirt was neatly tucked inside his pants that were fitted on his sacrum, very much below his waist, which was below his posterior. They were just barely hanging a few inches away from his intergluteal cleft, which is the way most teenage boys wear their pants today as a style. What made him exceptional was that his underwear was never shown. I was completely baffled since it was something that I had never seen before. It made me much more determined to find out a lot more about him.

CHAPTER TWO:
UNDER SUSPICION

EVERYTHING WAS BEGINNING TO CHANGE RAPIDLY. MY OTHER three aunts had already left home. The only aunt was left behind was preparing to get married with plans of taking my sister and me along, but my main focus was on high school.

There I was that Monday morning, dapperly clad in a pair of khaki shorts and a short-sleeved khaki shirt with epaulets pinned onto each shoulder of the shirt. My socks were pulled up to my knees with my feet neatly slipped into a pair of red bottom shoes which had a striking resemblance to a Christian Louboutin shoe, sent by my mom. With my bag over my shoulder, I slipped my black plastic frame, 50's style fashion nerdy glasses over my eyes then raced down to the first floor where my sister was awaiting me. "You look like an inspector," she said, which was something that I couldn't deny due to my khaki uniform having epaulets on both shoulders that were very similar to an inspector's uniform. I responded with a shrug and slipped a sandwich inside my bag before we both headed out the door.

Finally, we arrived in the vibrant city of Kingstown bustling with scores of children neatly dressed in various colored uniforms, crossing sidewalks and pedestrian crossings as frustrated drivers honked their horns in slow-moving traffic directed by a uniformed police officer. The wide-open gate of my new school was flocked by neatly dressed students and excited parents and guardians who smiled and greeted many as they walked by. I calmly exited the vehicle and took a moment to scan the faces of as many students as I possibly could in search of any familiar faces, but I couldn't seem to find any. Making my way onto the premises where batches of students chatted and introduced themselves, I found an isolated area where I quietly stood in observation for the rest of the morning until my eyes met a group of boys slapping the heads of every boy and tapping the shoulder of every girl as they passed. "Not again," I said to myself, knowing that could cause an altercation, which I always tried to avoid at every cost.

Just as the bell rang, a male teacher approached the gate with a massive lock in his hand, closed it, then clamped it onto the latch of the gate that caused it to produce such a loud clamping sound that I thought for a moment I saw a prisoner entering his cell as the door shut behind him. "Wow! Now I'm locked in here for the next five hours," I said to myself, knowing how uncomfortable I'd feel. Just thinking of a massive lock clamp onto a high school gate that prevented you from seeing the outside gave me the mentality of being caged in and caused me to wonder if it was a psychological attempt to keep us, students in check.

Bit by bit, teachers and students emerged from every direction and assembled in the middle of the schoolyard. The headmaster walked toward us in a distinctive walk that couldn't be ignored, then there was sudden dead silence as he scanned the faces of every new student until his eyes met my eyes. I was too nervous to look back at him and broke the stare by removing my glasses from my eyes and pretending that I was cleaning them. In his husky tone, he said, "Good morning all. Please close your eyes as we pray." I placed my glasses back over my eyes and closed them until the short prayer ended.

He then gave us an introduction that caused many to suck their teeth, roll their eyes and yawn. Many may consider the behavior to be disrespectful, but I found it to be quite justifiable. After all, it was our first day of high school and after coming off a long vacation, the last thing anyone wanted to hear was a long boring speech or to be asked if we had any past relatives who attended the school.

Fortunately for us, a drizzle commenced. As everyone scattered, I found myself unfortunately trapped inside the tumult and consequently got to my classroom late. Every seat toward the front of the class was already occupied. I sucked my teeth, shook my head, then made my way toward the back of the class where I never wanted to sit out of fear that I may not be able to hear the teacher loudly enough. There was also the possibility of some truth in the simple old saying that "anyone who sits at the back of the classroom never learns anything."

That day after I returned home, I began to think of the new location that I was moving to and wasn't sure how much

I'd like it. Although it was only a five-minute drive away, I felt more comfortable knowing that I was already surrounded by everything that was considered to be convenient, such as shops, the post office, the police station, school, churches, the playing field, and the beach. All were a two-minute walk, except for the beach, which was five minutes by foot. But my aunt thought that it was best to take my sister and me along with her.

The new location was situated on a hill that overlooked our previous neighborhood and was almost 400 meters further away from the main road. Walking up the hill several times a day through the merciless, mid-day sun was like a suicide mission. It left many exhausted, hungry, and dehydrated, and anyone with any respiratory health issues was left panting for air.

My sister and I were welcomed by everyone in the neighborhood. We quickly adjusted to everything, and after years of settling in, enjoyed countless adventures from crashing numerous parties and weddings to climbing trees and rocks where simple falls could have led to many deaths. We played soccer matches in areas where winning a game could have caused our entire team to be trapped with each man left to find his own escape route. These were challenges and adventures that I had never experienced growing up in Calliaqua, and I loved every minute of it. It was like a new beginning for me.

I had gotten so used to my mother not being around that all of the pain I felt after her departure had completely disappeared–until one night when she called and informed us that she was about to get married. Although it's been about four years since she'd migrated, knowing how soft, quiet, and kind-hearted she was, my curiosity peaked at a level of concern. "Who was this man? Where was he from?" were two questions I asked myself. I soon found out that he was a man of Caribbean descent whose parents were from an island not too far from St. Vincent and the Grenadines. Everyone, from my relatives to my mother's friends who knew her back in St. Vincent, all said that he appeared to be a wonderful man. The only person who thought differently of him was her uncle. I wasn't sure if it was due to his Navy training or his instinct but according to him, from the moment they met, he thought that there was something mysterious about the man my mother was about to marry, and he wasted no time in informing her that she needed to be careful.

Days leading up to the wedding, I finally had the opportunity to speak with him by phone and tried my best to match an image to his voice. My imagination of him was that of a man wearing glasses, slim built just like my father, but probably a little taller. Even though picturing him perfectly was impossible, one thing I discovered during our short conversation was that he spoke very fast and wasn't a great listener. It was as if he was only listening just to respond instead of listening attentively to what a person had to say. He constantly interrupted me by saying, "Yeah, yeah, yeah" while I was speaking and never allowed me the opportunity to complete my sentence. I perceived him to be impatient and overly controlling to an extent. Since my mother avoided altercations by simply agreeing to everything a person said, my instinct told me that she was in for much more than she was bargaining for.

It wasn't too long after that we received a photograph of him dressed in a suit and smiling with my mother standing beside him, wearing her wedding gown. Everything that I had imagined about him was the complete opposite of reality. He seemed a bit stern with a fake smile and for some strange reason, I had the idea that his body language indicated some form of deception. Although it was impossible to mentally scan his image for any evidence, from that moment it was as if there was just something about him that didn't appear genuine to me.

One night during a phone conversation just a few months into their marriage, everything appeared normal until my mother raced off the phone as if something was wrong. Although there wasn't anything to panic about, I was under the expectation that she would have returned the call the following day, but she never did. Weeks went by without any form of communication, which led me to be concerned, but I said nothing about it to anyone. At that time, there wasn't any access to softwares such as WhatsApp or VOIP. Making international calls from the Caribbean was like a punishment imposed by the only telephone company at the time that took advantage of everyone in the region for using their services. Their bills were outrageous, and they had no explanation for such injustice, but having no competition at the time caused them to do whatever they pleased.

After about a month of not hearing from my mother, she finally called and apologized for not reaching out much sooner and more often. I wasn't buying it. I was still under the suspicion that something just wasn't right, but responded "ok", casually. Three minutes into our conversation when I was about to hand the phone over to my sister, my mother said she had to go. "Wait, my sister is here," I said, but then heard a dial tone. "What?!" I asked myself as I stood there in silence, still baffled, holding the receiver in the palm of my hand, trying to make sense of what just happened. My sister, who was just feet away and engaged in her homework, was very much unaware of what took place. I decided that it was best not to alarm her but in the back of my mind, I was putting everything under observation. Everything pondered in my mind. From the time she called to the length of time spent on the phone, down to the sound of her voice, but I decided that it was best not to say anything to anyone.

Weeks went by before she made another phone call and for the third time, she ended the call within less than five minutes. To me, everything was now of significance. Even though I was unaware of her monthly expenses, it wasn't enough to convince me that she was piling with extra bills, and needed to decrease the number of phone calls made to us. She now had a husband, which to me means an additional income, which meant she would either continue to make the same number of phone calls she made before marrying him or the number of phone calls made would have increased. They would have never decreased. I also knew that she wasn't the extravagant type who wasted money to impress anyone so unless her husband had multiple debts, multiple expenses, or was unemployed, something had to be wrong.

Christmas was only days away, and the streets throughout Kingstown were vibrant and bustling. Shoppers swarmed stores and sidewalks as Christmas carols blared across the airwaves. Many were receiving barrels, crates, boxes, and Christmas cards complete with cash tucked inside, but my sister and I still hadn't received anything from our mother.

I had no access to the P.O. box but decided to peer through the keyhole and saw a pile of postcard-size envelopes stacked upon each other. Convinced that one of them had to be from her, I went home that day pretty much exhausted after walking through the sweltering sun that I somehow dozed off for a few hours. Suddenly, I was awakened by the jangling sound of keys as my aunt entered the house. "Anything for me?" I asked. "Yeah," she said, then pulled a stack of mail from her bag and handed it to me. I was stunned after realizing that they were all from my aunts who were living in another state. "Strange," I said to myself, then shook my head in disappointment. This was very much unusual. Before my mother's marriage, she had never missed calling or sending us anything for our birthdays, Christmas and even at Easter. To clear my mind, I hopped onto my bicycle and rode off into the evening sun as the warmth of the breeze hit my face and gently whistled into my ear that I felt the relaxation of a quiet serenity that was unexplainable. On my way back, that peace turned into a panic that almost cost me my life.

As I approached a steep hill, I changed the gear on my bicycle to allow myself to pedal easier. A snap immediately occurred. I thought nothing of it, and continued but out of curiosity, scanned the back wheel for any mechanical failure, and found nothing to be out of the ordinary. Just as I got to the top of the hill and was about to descend onto a second hill, I changed the gear for a second time and listened for the repeated sound of the snap, but there wasn't any sound. I went into my descent, pedaling as fast as I could, dancing the bicycle from side to side on the empty street when all of a sudden, my eyes met a truck approaching at a distance. As a precaution, I tested my brake and was shocked to know that there wasn't any. "What in the world," I cried out to myself with my eyes widened in complete panic. To make sure I wasn't daydreaming, I pressed the brake for a second time, and there still wasn't any response. With my eyes on the truck, I watched as it appeared and disappeared behind a grove of trees from time to time while still moving toward me. Knowing the speed at which I was traveling meant that there was a strong possibility of us reaching the corner simultaneously. I needed to avoid a collision by getting there first, and without hesitation, I switched into a faster gear, crouched myself onto the seat like a professional cyclist, and pedaled as fast as I could as the bicycle accelerated. Realizing that the excessive speed at which I was traveling meant that I couldn't turn the corner, panic set in for a second time. The thought of dragging my feet onto the pavement to slow the bicycle down crossed my mind, but the pair of sandals I was wearing wasn't any match for the pavement. My only escape was up a driveway located around the corner, up a hill on the opposite side of the street where a sign read "Trespassers will either be prosecuted by the owner or be eaten by dogs." At that moment, I was very much willing to take the chance of being eaten alive by dogs or shot instead of having my body transformed into minced meat on the pavement after being hit by a 3-ton truck.

I burst around the corner, leaning the bicycle as low as possible and watched as it drifted onto the opposite side of the street toward the approaching truck. Suddenly, the driver took notice of me and instantly jammed the brake, tooting his horn continuously with a deafening sound that scared me to death and caused me to twitch. The bicycle wobbled, but I managed to maintain control as the truck skidded toward me with screeching tires, leaving smoke behind as a hot puff of air slapped my body like a stiff buff of wind. I regained control of the bicycle and pedaled as fast as I could, racing toward the driveway. Then, with accurate timing, I lined the bicycle up with the driveway. I wedged myself about six feet between the driveway and the truck, then closed my eyes as tightly as possible to avoid any form of flashback if I ever survived the impact. A rush of adrenaline surged through my body as the bicycle rocketed up the driveway before it crashed onto the pavement, and left me sprawled motionless inside the yard. Within an instant, dogs were barking and out of panic, I opened my eyes to see two of them racing toward me. But my body had already given up, and I was unable to move. I closed my eyes in preparation to be eaten alive, then heard a woman scream from the top of her lungs, "Stop!" Everything ceased. There was complete silence as I barely opened my eyes and saw that both dogs were quietly seated just a few feet away with their eyes locked onto me. "Inside, now!" the woman continued walking toward me. As both dogs moved towards the back and disappeared, she approached me. "I saw the whole thing, and you're very lucky that I was home," I responded with a loud sigh, which indicated that I had just barely dodged two bullets. "Are you ok? Do you want some water or something?" she continued, but my trembled lips didn't allow me to respond. I shook my head "No."

Soon after, the driver, who was a large man, struggled to make his way up the driveway, panting as if he was in desperate need of oxygen. His eyes and mouth opened in shock after noticing that I was uninjured. "Man, I swear you were dead. I thought I ran over you, but after I didn't see any blood, I thought the truck tossed you into the bushes," he said frantically with both hands on his head. I responded with a stare, then he assisted me onto my feet only to watch me fall right back onto the pavement. Suddenly, I was able to speak and said, "Brake went out," and he replied, "I knew it had to be." I looked at the lady and said, "Thank you." The driver assisted me with the bicycle back down the driveway and onto the street. "You sure you're ok?" he asked, and I nodded, "Yes'' without any eye contact. As he made his way back into his truck and drove off, I hopped back onto the bicycle, but my knees were too numbed for me to pedal, and I fell onto the pavement like a sack of potatoes. "Take your time, and be careful" the woman shouted, and I responded with a wave before pushing the bicycle along.

Two weeks after, it was my birthday. Quietly seated at my desk in class, I began to wonder why up to that moment, neither my sister nor I had received any calls, Christmas cards, or my birthday card from our mother. Then out of nowhere, it was as if I was physically attacked by a migraine. My eyes became blurry and I felt as though I wanted to throw up. I closed my eyes and reclined in my seat with my head resting on the wall behind me, hoping that it would ease the pain, but there wasn't any relief. A few moments later, I regained perfect vision and approached the teacher who was seated at her desk. "Can I go home, please?", I asked. Without even asking what the problem was, she said "Weren't you just ok a few minutes ago?" I found the question to be quite foolish and stood there confused for a moment, realizing how much education and common sense are two completely different things. "How stupid," I thought to myself, knowing that everything must have a starting point. For example, a person could be having a conversation with you at one moment then two seconds later, fall into a cardiac arrest. There has to be a starting point leading up to that cardiac arrest, whether or not we are aware of such an unfortunate situation. I looked her in the eyes and then calmly said, "I have chronic migraines that suddenly come on." Then she asked, "Today is your birthday, isn't it?"

"It is, but it's not the reason why I want to leave," I responded. After realizing that my plea was only moving toward a debate, I stormed out of the classroom in anger as everyone watched in shock and murmured amongst themselves, and barged inside the headmaster's office. I had forgotten to knock on his office door, and he looked at me with his eyes widened as if he'd seen a ghost. I explained the problem to him, without any questions, I was allowed to leave. Out of anger and loss of respect for the teacher, I grabbed my bag without saying a word, and left the school premises like an intoxicated man, staggering from side to side as my head pounded.

As my head pounded, I hopped onto a minibus, and moved toward a window to the rear in case I needed to throw up, and quietly reclined on the seat as my head banged against the seat from every wild turn the driver who was no more than 25 years of age made from his reckless driving. Twenty minutes later, we made a stop at the post office in the area where I grew up. As passengers exited, I saw the woman who was in charge of the post office seated on a chair outside with her arms folded and her eyes blankly staring toward the ground and thought to myself, "Perhaps she's bored," Just then, the driver informed me that it was his final stop, and I needed to exit the bus. The migraine pounded harder, and harder as I staggered off the minibus and onto the platform of the post office. I became so dizzy for the second time and almost passed out, but managed to stagger toward the wall where I leaned for support. With the palm of my hand rested on my forehead, I helplessly sat on the floor with my eyes closed and the back of my head rested on the wall like a vagrant. There was constant chattering and murmuring all around me, but no one came to my aid. After it became overbearing, I hopped back onto a second minibus then staggered home through the sweltering sun as the heat penetrated my khaki uniform.

My thoughts were still on my birthday card as I entered the house, but was once again disappointed after noticing that it still hadn't arrived. With my head shaking in disappointment, I released a sigh, pulled my knapsack from over my back, then sprawled onto the floor with my eyes closed. It wasn't until I was awakened by my aunt that I realized I had slept for almost six consecutive hours. "Any mail?" I asked her, and she responded, "No." "Strange," I said to myself, then glanced at the clock on the wall and saw that it was close to 8 p.m. To ease my mind, I reminded myself that the night was still young and that most overseas calls came in at around 10 p.m. At 9:45 p.m., I glanced back and forth from time to time between the television and the solid red light embedded in the telephone that I was hoping to see flash at any moment. It never did. I reclined inside the chair with my eyes closed, still patiently awaiting my mother's phone call. Hours passed, and the thought that the phone never rang made me realize that something had to be wrong. This was my birthday, a day that my mother would have never missed calling me. Even though I couldn't pinpoint exactly what it was wrong, there was no doubt in my mind that her husband had something to do with her not calling me that night.

It was nearing 11 p.m. and out of frustration, I had enough. After releasing a loud sigh, I exited the house into the dead of night and entered the veranda where I quietly sat on the step with my chin in the palm of my hand. Through the still of partial moonlight obstructed by the branches of an overhead tree, I stared at the pulsing lights of fireflies, not even disturbed by the constant chirping of crickets. Out of nowhere, a silhouette of the dog emerged from the darkness with his tail wiggling. His eyes beamed like two brilliant, mini headlamps. The more he approached, I ignored his existence, but he wasn't taking no for an answer. After sensing my sorrow, he chose to console me by rubbing his hairy body against me, and I had no choice but to cuddle him and gently brush the hair on his back with the palm of my hand. It didn't take long for me to bid him goodbye as he quietly stared at me in silence with his tail wiggling.

Upon re-entering the house, I stopped one final time inside the doorway. With my eyes glued onto the solid, red light on the telephone one last time, I was hoping to see it transformed into a pulsing blue light. Instead, the reality of my mother not calling finally struck me. I found a seat on the floor in complete silence and stared vacantly at the nearby cashew tree lit by the brilliant moonlight. There, I quietly wished myself a happy birthday and awoke the following morning with my eyes staring at the break of dawn.

It took me a while to put myself together before entering the vehicle with my arms folded, looking through the window with glazed eyes for the entire journey until a hand tapped me on the shoulder. "Your stop," someone beside me said, and I snapped out of it. After exiting the vehicle, a classmate who saw a change in my demeanor approached me. "Wappen?" he asked, which is a Caribbean term for asking "What happened?" "Nutten," I calmly replied as we made our way into the classroom. My brain immediately went blank. I lost concentration and began to fidget, sigh, and quietly sucked my teeth from time to time, and had no idea what was taking place during any of my classes. It wasn't until on my break, and most of the students exited the class that I regained focus.

Overtaken by hunger, I reached inside my bag in search of my sandwich only to realize that it wasn't there, then I released a loud sigh, sucked my teeth in frustration, and laid my head on the desk hoping that it would end my frustration. Hunger suddenly got the worst of me and caused my stomach to growl loudly like an angry animal. To avoid embarrassment, I got to my feet like a man still in slumber and made my way toward the cafeteria where I reluctantly joined a long line as I continued to suck my teeth and shake my head from time to time. After being served a drink inside a plastic cup along with a pastry wrapped inside a napkin, on my way back to my classroom, the same group of boys who on the first day of school were tapping the shoulder of every girl and slapping the heads of every boy who passed beside them were standing about 20 feet away, idled inside the corridor. My previous encounter with them left me in anger after being slapped to the back of my head and my glasses fell from my face onto the pavement. Instead of fighting back, I calmly picked them up, placed them back over my eyes, stared at each boy in silent anger as my blood gushed through my body, then without saying a word quietly proceeded toward my classroom. But I vowed never to allow it to happen again.

For a moment, I contemplated my next move, knowing that I had already gotten into a fight back in primary school. To avoid any altercation, I decided to reroute into a different classroom where I was quickly stopped by a "Prefect" who acted as if the classroom was a piece of land handed down to him by his ancestors. "Hey, you. You just can't walk through here like that whenever you want to," he said. I replied, "My classroom is just here," pointing toward it 12 inches away and separated by only a partition with no door. "I don't care," he replied. As much as I was tempted to proceed, something as simple as that could have landed me inside the headmaster's office so to avoid anything, I shook my head and calmly exited his classroom. Stepping back into the corridor, one of the notorious boys and I locked eyes. His mouth broadened into the most mischievous grin ever as he tapped on the shoulder of one of his boys before they all burst out giggling like a pack of hungry Hyenas. There wasn't any fear inside of me, and neither was there any submission. Instead, I walked toward them, increasing my pace. Just as I passed the first boy, a slap connected to the back of my head. I quickly turned in anger to look at the perpetrator and just as I did, I was instantly mobbed and attacked from every direction. Slaps connected to every part of my head. Clumps of pastries flew from out of my hand and landed everywhere as my drink splattered to the floor. My glasses ripped from my face and hit the ground. I went completely berserk, swinging both of my fists uncontrollably in every direction, and heard knuckles knock against bodies but had absolutely no idea where they connected. Someone threw a punch toward my face and with quick reflexes, I ducked out of the way. The punch missed my face and connected to the back of my neck, caused me to burst into a bigger rage, and aimed for the stomach of the boy who was standing closest to me then with all of my strength, drove a karate punch straight into the middle of his stomach. "Oh", he yelled, holding his stomach as he staggered back onto the wall and crouched to the ground in agony before he grunted in pain like a little girl. Out of nowhere, the same Prefect who stopped me from entering his classroom pulled us apart. I was puffing like an angry animal, staring at each boy with my fist folded and ready to go to round two if needed. Our once neatly tucked-in shirts were out of our pants. They were ruffled with buttons and epaulets, ripped from off them and my glasses rested on the floor twisted with broken lenses. With my fist still folded, I said in an intimidating tone, "Someone's paying for this or there will be a round two."

"I should very well demand that all of you go inside the headmaster's office now!" the Prefect said but off the bat, I reminded him that the entire brawl could have been avoided had he allowed me to pass through his classroom. He never replied. Without saying another word, I retrieved my glasses from the ground, then re-entered my classroom.

That evening, I got home, hungry and tired then raided the refrigerator and cupboard in search of something to eat but being a picky eater, I couldn't find anything worth devouring. The thought of my neighbor coming from behind his house every day with his hands loaded with eggs crossed my mind. No matter how much we pleaded with him to show us the location, he never disclosed the hiding place. Like Elmer Fudd on a rabbit hunt, I went out on an egg search that took me beneath every nearby tree and through patches of high grass almost five feet tall. Out of nowhere, an angry hen launched at me with her wings extended like an eagle. After escaping her attack with a brisk, I backed out of sight to conceal myself as she scanned the surroundings in search of me to no avail. Suddenly, she moved away, which allowed me to cautiously emerge from my hiding place, snatched all six eggs, then raced into the house and consumed at least three of them.

Hours later while seated in the chair, my neighbor who I'll call Spottie arrived from school, still neatly dressed with his knapsack over his back. He headed straight for the fowl nest, then came to a sudden stop as his knapsack jolted over his back. With his eyes open in shock, he frantically scanned the surroundings in disappointment. "Bo, bo, bo boy, who moved all the eggs?" he stuttered before he flung both hands into the air as he sighed. "You me mean to te tell me that they couldn't even le leave one?" he continued. I thought to myself, "Who inside of their right mind would raid a fowl nest without taking everything," but later, came to find out that removing all the eggs causes the fowl never to return to the exact spot.

Unexpectedly, he looked in my direction, and was convinced that I was the culprit since I was the only person in the area who attended the only high school on the island that began at 8:15 a.m. and ended at 1:15 p.m, while all the others ended at 3:00 p.m. As much as I wanted to burst out laughing, I managed to control myself. Fortunately for him, the following day while he and I along with a few others in the neighborhood were playing a game of football, I accidentally kicked the ball away. Upon retrieving it, I came across a second fowl nest loaded with eggs. My eyebrows raised with excitement. I smiled, then raced back to everyone whining, "I just saw a nest full of eggs." Everyone's eyes lit up. We looked at each other before we looked toward a 70-plus-year-old man who was seated at the entrance of his doorway. "The property isn't his, and neither are the eggs," one person said. Our main concern was to make sure that the man was not alerted in any way since at times he appeared to be very loud and obnoxious, and had a habit of making things worse than they were. Everyone looked at me as if I was responsible for coming up with a master plan. A lightbulb suddenly went off inside my head, and I said "Ok, one of you kick the ball as close as possible toward the nest. As I go to pick it up, I'll remove as many eggs as I possibly can, but this time, I'll make sure that I leave one behind." After a short discussion, I was chosen to kick the ball. What?", I burst out. My reputation as a sportsman was already tarnished after I bowled a ball in the previous game of cricket that resulted in the shattering of a street light and an unforgettable whip from my grandfather. Realizing that the guys still somehow had faith in me, I had the opportunity to regain my reputation. "Ok", I said. I took one final glance toward the house and saw that the elderly man was still seated at the entrance of the doorway with his back turned toward us, then placed the ball at a perfect spot on the ground, stepped back, and slowly jogged toward it with confidence. Like a world class football player, I kicked the ball with the arch of the bottom of my foot and watched it soar into midair. Everyone uttered "Oohs" and "Ahhs" as we mimicked our bodies to the curve of the ball. For a moment, it was as if the ball hovered in midair. We used the opportunity to glance back at the elderly man who was still seated at the entrance of his doorway and was still unaware of what was taking place. Just as I turned my attention back toward the ball, it dropped onto the ground, rolled exactly into the nest, and came to a complete stop. Our eyes lit up as we looked at each other with our mouths open in shock before we erupted in laughter, bumped fists, and high-fived each other. What excited me most was that I had regained my reputation as a sportsman. The elderly man was still in complete oblivion, and without alarming him, we took as many eggs as we could, but this time, left one behind.

Time was moving rapidly, and over a month had passed since anyone had communicated with my mother. Out of curiosity, I decided that it was time to give her a call. The phone rang constantly for a moment before she finally answered in a dull tone. Her voice was disguised, and during our conversation, I noticed that she was very brief with a "Yes" or "No" response. Suddenly, someone mumbled in the background, and in that instant, she said, "I have to go now" and ended the call. It was obvious to me that the person in the background had very much indicated to her that she needed to end the conversation. For a moment, I stood in complete silence, baffled as to why she never even mentioned anything about whether she sent me a birthday or Christmas card, but still decided to give her the benefit of the doubt since there was a strong possibility that the mail could have been delayed, which happened quite often. There was also the possibility that she may have sent the mail to the post office in the area where I previously lived, which was something she did several times. I decided to check the post office for the second time. Upon my arrival, the mail van had just pulled in with a sack of mail, and after lingering with friends at the nearby playing field for about an hour and a half, I figured it was time to check. At first, I approached the platform under the building and stopped a few feet away out of sight as I pondered whether to enter or not. Even though I knew that it was my right to check for mail whenever needed, I wanted to make sure that the woman over the counter wasn't being aggravated in any way due to my frequent visits. After realizing that I was only doing my own investigation on my mother, I entered the post office. As soon as the lady saw me, she said "There isn't anything here for you." "Ok, thank you," I said, then calmly made my exit.

Unable to sleep that night, I called my mother the following day, expecting the phone to ring. Instead, I was greeted with a recording that said, "Sorry, the number you called has been changed." "What?!" I said to myself. Thinking that I had accidentally dialed the wrong number, I manually redialed the number and was greeted with the same message. "Why would my mother change her number without informing any of her family?" I asked myself. It was something that left me puzzled and didn't make any sense to anyone.

For weeks numerous calls were made to her, and every unanswered call greeted me with the same message: "Sorry, the number you called has been changed." I was distraught, and thought about her nonstop, and was very much worried. About a month later, she suddenly called and tried her best to pretend as if everything was ok but what I heard during the conversation was a nervous woman who knew that she was taking a chance to make a phone call. I asked, "Are you ok?" "Yeah," she replied, then gave me her new telephone number and insisted that I call at a specific time. No time before or no time later. "Strange," I thought but said nothing about it. Convinced that she wanted me to call at a time when her husband wasn't at home, I was still willing to break the rule and call at a much later time in order to get to the truth.

At about 11:15 a.m. once a week I called, and noticed that each time the calls ended at a particular time. It got to a point when I thought that it was time for me to break the rule, and decided to call at least 45 minutes later just to see what would happen. When I did, her husband answered, which confirmed my suspicion that I was only allowed to call the house when he wasn't at home. As much as I wanted to hang the phone up, the way he answered in a fake, deep, dominant tone grabbed my attention, and I decided to hang on. "Hey, good afternoon," I said, then identified myself. To my surprise, his tone of voice got deeper and sounded as if he wanted to assert some form of authority over me. "Your mother is unable to come to the phone now, but I'll let her know that you called," he said. I purposely paused for a moment, expecting him to prolong the conversation for at least a minute or two since the only time we spoke was just a few weeks before their marriage. But the same man who babbled on the phone and didn't even allow me to speak ended the call in just a few seconds. I was very much under the impression that my mother was nearby but was very much unable to come to the phone.

The following day, she called at 11:20 a.m., five minutes later than she told me to call her, which left me puzzled. It didn't take long for me to figure out why after hearing someone breathing not too far away or perhaps on a separate line. Pretending that I was unaware of the breathing, I was convinced that the purpose of her calling was all instigated by him to see if anyone had a habit of speaking to her at a time when he wasn't at home. I kept the conversation casual, but after all her responses were "Yes" and "No," it was another indication that she couldn't speak to anyone whenever he was around, and I realized it was time to hang up the phone and did.

The next day, I got out of bed agitated, paced the floor back and forth constantly, as I wondered whether to call her or not. Finally, I decided that it was best to call on the weekend at a time when I believe that her husband was home, in order to give him the impression that I wasn't only calling when he wasn't around. My aunt's phone bill was racking up, but she somehow understood my reason for making those calls, and as much as I felt her pain, I couldn't delay any longer since I was only conducting my personal investigation. Constraining myself from making those calls was very difficult, but I still needed to use my own discretion. After a moment, I reached for the phone and dialed the number but before it rang, I hung up. For some reason, I wasn't convinced that I needed to make a call just yet. After exiting the house to calm myself down, I laid on the grass for a moment with my head battling against everything. I just couldn't get over the fact that everything was weird and out of character for a man to be acting that way. Finally, I re-entered the house, made the call, and was expecting him to answer this time. Instead, I was greeted with a second unexpected message: "Sorry, the number you called has been changed." With the receiver still inside my hand, I closed my eyes and sighed, hung the phone up, then sat on the floor with my head buried between my legs in silence. Out of concern, I called one of my aunts who was living in another state, and informed her of all the strange activity that was just too much for me to bear. To confirm that I was correct, she dialed the number and got the same message. Out of concern, a letter was mailed to my mother, only to have it returned unopened, stamped "Return to sender." "Did my mother move again without informing anyone, or was she in a position where she was too afraid to answer?" I wondered. Everything had me confused. Convinced she was manipulated by a man who had an obsession with control, I realized the only way for anyone to get back in touch with her was to sit and wait and hope that she'd call.

CHAPTER THREE:
THE ABSENCE

MY YEARS OF HIGH SCHOOL HAD JUST COMPLETED AND THE annual Carnival festivity had already commenced, with costumes displayed everywhere. Streets and sidewalks were swarmed by foreigners and returnees who joined with the locals and partied to the soca music that blared the airwaves.

It was time for me to take the next step, and I began to reflect on life. Being self-employed was always my first option since I always wanted to have the independence of traveling the world, mixing with other cultures, and making a difference in parts of Africa and the Caribbean, mainly in Haiti. Several plans were put in place to make this possible, but three stood out. Becoming a musician was my first option. My second was to start a clothing line, and my third option was to become a pilot and start a chartering service throughout the islands of the Grenadines, which are all to the south of mainland St. Vincent. If all failed, then I wanted to become a criminal defense attorney and establish a law firm or work as an FBI agent. Since being a musician was my first love, I needed to sharpen my piano skills. There were several musicians in my family, including my great aunt, who taught many how to play the piano but she had already passed away. As much as I wanted her to teach me before she passed, I was scared after seeing how often she pounded her students' knuckles with a baton whenever they made a mistake. My father, who many considered to be one of the greatest pianists on the island had already migrated. His father, who taught him and many others how to play, was still the organist at the Anglican Church where I was an altar boy, and since he was also a tailor, I realized that I had a better advantage over many and decided to kill two birds with one stone. One night I approached him and told him that I needed to improve my piano skills and also wanted to learn how to sew. Before answering, he looked me deep into the eyes for a moment and then asked, "How serious are you?" "Very," I replied. "You're sure about that?" he continued to ask. "Yes, I am," I replied, then watched him bob his head continuously with his eyes glued to me in silence. "Report to me at 11 a.m. on Monday," he said, and I replied, "Ok." That Monday, I showed up at 9 a.m. to observe the tailors' work on their assigned machines, and one of them informed me that it wasn't that difficult to use. At 11 a.m., my grandfather walked through the door, looked at me, and smiled. "I see you're already here," he said. "Yeah, since 9 a.m.," I responded. "Then maybe you should come in at this time from now on, then at 11 a.m., you can come upstairs and start your piano lessons," he said. "Sure," I replied. He handed me several pieces of cloth sketched with buttonholes and a needle and asked that I stitch around them all by hand. I looked at him and then asked, "Can't the machine do this?" He replied, "This is how it was done before there were any machines." At that point, I knew that it wasn't going to work because I wasn't going to do something by hand that could simply be done on a machine that was available and capable of doing the same thing. To me, it was like having a computer at hand but chose to use a typewriter instead. "Man, why do you have him making buttonholes by hand?" one of the tailors asked with a giggle, and my grandfather quickly reminded him that everyone needed to learn from the beginning, then walked away. I sighed and shook my head, then within the second week, I just couldn't continue. To me, there wasn't any point in doing it. At 11 a.m., I took the stairs up to the second floor where he was already seated at the piano awaiting me, and quietly sat beside him then began to play, but couldn't concentrate due to my mind battling the decision of telling him that I no longer wanted to continue the sewing, without hurting his feelings. The fact that he was so dedicated to his work meant that whatever he did was taken seriously. I knew that once I told him I wanted to quit, it was going to upset him. During my piano session, I began to make countless mistakes that I normally never made and he quickly realized, and asked, "Are you ok?", and I answered, "Yeah," but it was quite obvious to him that I wasn't concentrating and he called it a wrap for the day. I took a deep breath, paused, turned toward him, and said, "I don't think that I want to continue sewing anymore." He looked at me without blinking, then I watched his demeanor change. There wasn't even a smirk on his face. The room went silent, except for the ticking of the clock, and it was quite obvious to me that he wasn't pleased with my decision. I was uncomfortable enough to break the silence and apologized, but he stared at me continuously with his head bobbing for a moment before he asked, "What made you change your mind?" "The button holes. I don't like making them by hand when all the machines can do the same thing," I said. "Everyone did it," he replied. I tried to explain to him that machines were like computers. They were invented to make our jobs and lives easier and faster. Then he asked, "What would happen if all of the machines that you were using happened to malfunction at the same time?" "The chances of such a thing happening are next to impossible," I responded, but a teenager trying to explain something to a person much older will most likely be to no avail. As he got to his feet, I saw the hurt inside of him and realized how important everything meant to him, but on the other hand, I was a teenager who wanted everything done the modern way.

After getting home that day, I found myself spreaded on the floor with my eyes fixed onto the ceiling, wondering if I had made the right decision since working for someone else was never my intention. Self-employment and independence were always my goals, and I thought that continuing to make buttonholes by hand might have allowed me to then master the machine, which could allow me to start my clothing line, but the constant thoughts of my mother running through my mind made it impossible for me to concentrate. I began to spend time with my 96-year-old great-grandmother who I was very much closer to in my younger years before she moved to a new location. Her mind was as sharp as a child's, and the way in which she related her childhood stories to me intrigued me and made me feel as if I was experiencing everything that she was speaking about. There were times when she was relating the stories to me, I closed my eyes and imagined myself living in the Caribbean at a time when there was no electricity, no telephones, and the main communication came from a radio that only worked with batteries during good weather conditions. At the time, the main means of transportation were wagons and donkeys which made me wish that I had such an experience to see what my life would have been like. Much of my time was spent with her, but one day while making plans to visit her after hearing that she was ill, I felt a bit tired after my return from spending a long day at Calliaqua and decided to rest for a while. Then my aunt broke the news to me that she had just passed. I froze with my lips sealed, sighed, then quietly shook my head. Although I didn't shed a tear, her memories left an everlasting impact on my life. Sadly enough, I didn't attend her funeral, which is something that I cannot forgive myself for and still bothers me whenever I think about it. I had no excuse for remaining at home that day due to my selfish attitude. I was a naive, teenage boy who thought that shedding tears at her funeral was a sign of weakness. Looking back at it now, my behavior showed that I was very much selfish and heartless not to give her the final respect she deserved.

With my eyes closed, and my head reclined on the couch, the frightened thought of losing my mother without seeing her one final time crossed my mind. It scared the living daylights out of me, so much that it made me realize that since I was her only son, it was my responsibility to resolve the entire mystery behind the madness. My first step was to find out if she had sent any recent mail, and I wasted no time doing so. I arrived at the post office and saw the lady quietly seated behind the counter. Her thoughts were completely far away, and I thought that she was probably a bit bored. "Good afternoon," I said. Without looking at me, she asked "How often are you going to come here?" Her question made me realize how much my frequent trips were aggravating her, and I calmly responded, "I have my reasons, and as soon as I figure out what's going on, you won't see me again." She looked at me for a moment and paused, then without saying another word handed me three envelopes separated from a pile. The first thing I noticed was that all the envelopes appeared warped with smudges of ink as if they were somehow damned by some form of a liquid, probably rain, and were all stamped months apart. As I continued to inspect each envelope, what grabbed my attention was the awkward handwriting on each envelope, which to me, suggested that they were probably written by a child or an adult who wasn't quite used to writing with a pen. There wasn't any return address on any of them, and they were all stamped in a small town that many had never heard of located almost 1,500 miles away from New York City and was barely visible on the U.S map. It was a place where you'd be lucky to find any Caribbean immigrant, unless they were probably on the run. I was very much puzzled and couldn't think straight as I stared at the envelopes, and tried to make sense of it all.

I returned home, and handed the letters over to my aunt who opened each one and noticed that they were all typed, except for my birthday card, which had a new telephone number written in the same awkward handwriting along with a message that was typed: "To my dearest son. Have a Merry Christmas, A happy New Year, and a happy birthday. Sorry I couldn't be with you, but I love you very much." Receiving such a birthday card about six months after my birthday made me wonder what could have caused such a delay. It immediately sent me into detective mode, and I began to scrutinize everything about those letters without even knowing what I was looking for.

The following day, I awoke with my eyes fixed on the ceiling, contemplating my next move. Just as my aunt left for work, I sprung to my feet, glanced at the clock from time to time, then as it struck 12:30 p.m., I reached for the phone but wasn't sure what time it was in the state where the mail arrived from. I quickly hung the phone up, then after a moment of pondering, took a deep breath, exhaled, then hesitantly reached for the telephone a second time before pulling my hand back at the last second as I shook my head in frustration and asked myself, "Should I do this?" A moment went by, then I reached for the telephone a second time, dialed the number, and instantaneously, my mother answered. It was as if she was awaiting my call. Without even saying good afternoon, I asked, "What is going on?" "I'm ok," she said. "No, you're not," I responded based on the crack in her voice. I wanted to pressure her into telling me what was happening, but instead, I sighed and informed her of her grandmother's death and that my sister had migrated, which caused her to break down. She apologized for not keeping in touch as often as she should, and the more she spoke, I felt pity toward her and couldn't ask anything about the returned mail or about her new address, all out of fear that she wasn't in any condition to answer certain questions.

Suddenly, the door squeaked and her voice trembled. Then in a deep voice, someone mumbled in an aggressive tone that caused her to whisper into the phone, then a clang occurred which made me realize that the phone wasn't properly hung up. I used the opportunity to eavesdrop and heard footsteps approaching the phone. The person mumbled for a second time in a very disturbed, dominant tone. Not once did my mother respond. She was scared and defenseless with no one to turn to. As much as I wanted to scream, I knew that doing so would have meant that she'd face all the consequences alone and her telephone number would have changed again in an instant.

Out of nowhere, my dog appeared and stood inside the doorway, wagging his tail as if he wanted to play. Out of fear that he'd blow my cover, I quickly reached for a half cup of tea left on the table by my aunt, splashed it onto the floor of the veranda, and watched the dog lick it up, then heard, "Hello," over the phone. I remained as quietly as possible. Not even the sound of my breathing was heard. The dog looked at me as if he wanted to bark for more. I took a piece of bread, tossed it as far as possible, and watched him race after it. Just then, a click occurred. Then the phone finally went dead.

The experience left me to assume that my mother's reason for not properly hanging the phone up was a desperate cry for help. That night, I couldn't sleep as everything played out inside my head like a movie. The following day, I called her and was expecting to hear "Sorry the number you called has been changed." Just as I heard "Sorry..." I was about to hang up, but for some reason decided to remain on the line instead, and heard a different message, "...the number you called has been disconnected or is no longer in service." "What!" I said to myself with my eyes widened in shock. "Oh my God," I continued and was sighing in panic. I paced the floor before I found a seat and buried my face in the palm of my head. It was as if my head was spinning out of control. I got back on my feet and frantically paced the floor back and forth restlessly and sighed continuously with my head shaking in anguish.

Within a few days, all the mail that was sent to her new address returned and for the second or third time, were all stamped, "Return to sender." I picked each one up for the second time, and like a detective, began to scrutinize them one after the other, curious as to what I could possibly find. Suddenly, my forehead began to pulse like a bass speaker. Everything in my sight became blurry and the constant thought of not knowing my mother's whereabouts for probably the millionth time intensified the pain.

CHAPTER FOUR:
CLUES TO A MISSING TRAIL

ABOUT FIVE YEARS WENT BY WITHOUT ANY FORM OF COMMUNIcation from my mother. Everything had ceased. It was as if she had vanished into thin air, and many family members presumed she was dead. "She's dead," one family member said constantly with a sad look on her face as she shook her head just before becoming despair. While many were under that assumption, I simply ignored it as much as possible and looked at everything through a different lens. There was still hope for me to prove to everyone that she wasn't dead, and I figured that it was time for me to attempt a rescue.

Out of desperation and without planning, I filled out a visa application, went through the proper procedures, and waited for a reply. In a few days, I was "denied" and was sent a letter that explained the reason for my rejection. Neither was I sad, upset, or disappointed in any way. After all, it was only done out of desperation. The rejection to me was like a learning experience. I decided to tape the letter onto the mirror of my dresser where I glanced at it daily to remind myself that as soon as the time was right, I needed to pick myself up and try again but needed to be very well prepared.

Everything was battling inside me. I did my best to keep it all together by trying to live normally, but to think that she was mentally abused constantly without anyone to turn to drove me nuts. To avoid thinking of it, all my nights were spent outdoors where I played dominoes with friends and neighbors, and watched movies at the nearby medical college, but after I returned home, all the memories reappeared. I prayed night after night and asked God to allow us to see her, even if it was for one final time before taking her, then just as I fell asleep, I had constant dreams about her that awoke me, then immediately vanished out of my memory. To me, they were all indications of a struggling woman trapped in a house and was desperately pleading for a way out. Getting back to sleep was most difficult for me, and I had no choice but to exit the house and step out into the veranda where I sometimes sat alone, and hoped that everything would all go away.

My days weren't any different. Being at home was more detrimental than anything else. There were times I pinched myself to make sure that I wasn't daydreaming or overthinking in any way. The dominant tone of her husband's voice played inside of my head. To look at the returned letters, and to think that her telephone numbers were constantly changing all reminded me that I wasn't overthinking the situation. I'd leave home to escape the pain only to be irritated by a constant barrage of questions from vacationers returning from

New York City. The first question was always, "Where is your mother? I haven't seen her in a long time. Is she still living in New York?" I'd always respond "No," then they'd always follow up the question by asking "So, where is she?" My response was always the same: "She's living in a state that you normally don't visit, thousands of miles away from New York," but the questioning never stopped. I had gotten so used to it that it was like reciting the dialogue of a play. It drove me completely insane. At times, it was as if I was cross-examined by a prosecutor for her disappearance. One day I almost exploded on someone after they met me on the street, and asked a question that I thought was out of line: "How come you haven't gone to meet your mother yet?" they asked. I thought that the question could have been asked in a much different way, but instead of responding, I shrugged my shoulders and gave a look that left them confused.

Out of anger, I returned home and hoped that my neighbors were, but unfortunately, none of them was. None of us had cell phones at the time, and it was very much impossible to know each other's whereabouts, but since school was on vacation, and there was nothing but cleared, blue sky, I was under the impression that they were most likely on a hidden beach called "Breakers" which wasn't at all tourist friendly due to its massive waves that pound the beach from the Atlantic side of the island. The beach was always difficult to access especially after it rained, but as teenagers, it was where we enjoyed playing football, fishing, and cooking during our school vacations.

I made my way down the narrow three-foot-wide pathway between a grove of trees littered with dry, discarded leaves as a stale, sulfur smell of the ocean lingered. I watched as the ocean angrily roared from through the open spaces of the trees as it produced enormous waves that splashed into white, bubbly water as it battered the black sandy beach, then receded with everything in its path. We were used to it, and were never scared since we all stayed at a safe distance during a certain season. For some reason, that day, my instinct insisted that I needed to return home. On the other hand, to return home would have only resulted in mental torture. I kept on moving down the hill before I suddenly came across several pieces of sticks that caught my attention. One piece for some reason stood out. It had the perfect height of a cane and was strong enough to sustain the weight of the average human. For some strange reason, I picked it up, inspected it, then tossed it aside not too far away from the path. After continuing on, I finally got onto the beach where about six or seven boys who I didn't recognize were all involved in a football game. "Anyone else apart from you all here?" I asked, "Nah," one of them replied and for the second time, Something told me that I needed to return home. "Nah", I said to myself after realizing how far I'd walked. It was only fair enough for me to enjoy a game of football. "You guys need another player?" I asked. "Yeah, yeah, play on that side," the same guy replied. I slipped my feet out of my sneakers and quickly got into position. Within an instant, someone kicked the ball into the air and I leaped with the intention of head-butting the ball, and was pushed from in front. The force of the push was so hard that it jerked my body backward. It felt as if I was hit by a vehicle. My life flashed before my eyes, and reminded me of the day when I was almost crushed by a truck while riding my bicycle. I almost cartwheeled in midair toward a death fall but managed to land on one knee. I heard "Clack, clack" like the sound of a shotgun barrel and felt my kneecap shift from side to side. I screamed in excruciating pain then threw myself onto the sand, landed on my back and screamed continuously. The pain was so intense that it caused me to grab a hold of my knee and bit onto my teeth as the unbearable pain continued. With the palm of my hand tightly grabbed onto my knee, I rolled from side to side, uncontrollably then tilted my head to glance at my knee which appeared to be the size of a mamey sapote. That's when the reality hit me that I should have never disobeyed my instinct.

One of the boys approached and asked if I was hurt, but his question was nothing more than a sham. He looked at me for about two seconds without saying another word before continuing the game. "This can't be real," I said to myself as I shook my head, helplessly, sprawled on my back with the palm of both hands still resting on my injured knee.

Moments later, I took notice that the sun was about to set, and was hovering at what appeared to be just feet away from the horizon. My knee was at a 90-degree angle as I came to a sitting position on the sand, just in time and saw the boys leaving. "Yo, help me," I yelled out, flinching in severe pain, but the sound of my screaming voice was overpowered by the angry roars of the ocean. I looked at the lush, vast wall of green mountain behind me, then sighed in hope that it was all hallucination, but the agonizing pain in my knee and the sound of the ocean, and its massive waves that battered the sand as the water drew nearer toward me, reminded me that it was all a reality and that I needed to leave.

It was only a matter of time before I was dragged into the water. Panic set in, and with the palm of one hand resting on the sand, I prised myself onto my uninjured knee and crawled toward an almond tree in search of anything capable to support my 120-pound frame. The constant, merciless pain quivered through my entire knee with vengeance for disobeying my instinct. Even though I found nothing to assist me, the roars of the ocean prompted me. I grabbed hold of the almond tree and slowly brought myself to stand on my uninjured knee, then hopped to a few feet only to fall back onto the sand where I moaned in pain.

Minutes by minute, the water drew nearer as a final reminder that I needed to leave. With one deep breath, I came to a sitting position for a second time, then dragged myself backward up the hill with my face flinched in unbearable pain that still wasn't severe enough to keep me trapped. My search for the cane I tossed aside earlier on was to no avail, and out of frustration, I screamed my lungs out in hope that someone would hear me, but no one did, and the more time elapsed, I came to realize that I was all on my own in what I considered to be the wilderness.

After I shook my head, I sighed before sucking my teeth, then found a seat on the root of a massive tree that branched through the earth like highly prominent veins. For the first time in months, I somehow found serenity. The wind had ceased. There wasn't even the chirping of a bird, and the distant roars of the angry ocean went simply on deaf ears. As much as I wanted to linger for as long as I possibly could, the reduction of sunlight didn't allow me to.

Suddenly, voila! The stick I was searching for was now in sight. With my eyes fixed on it and a broad smile from ear to ear, I laughed, then dragged myself about 15 feet back down the hill, retrieved it, before bringing myself to a standing position on my uninjured knee, only to realize that my injured knee was quite stiff and heavier, had a burning sensation that quivered through my meniscus. With my head shaking, and like a man seven decades older than my age, I limped my way out of the wilderness until I reached a residential neighborhood before I stopped to release a loud sigh as I took the moment to look back at the sun, which was halfway submerged beyond the horizon, partially concealed by patches of clouds that reflected into the sky like a fiery sunset.

As the moment slipped by, I limped my way around a corner, then found myself completely frozen inside my tracks with my eyes widened in shock, staring at four neighborhood dogs who quietly napped on the pavement like a group of gangsters. "What in the world did I do to deserve all this?" I asked myself as I pondered my only escape, which was a 10-minute walk up an unpaved hill littered with gravel. It had no street light, and the thought of stepping on any loose gravel in the dark meant that there was a possibility that I could have caused injury to my uninjured knee. With such dangerous obstruction, my only choice was to face the dog.

The stick in my hand was my only aid, but to the dogs, it appeard as a weapon. Although it was my only defense, after about ten decisive seconds of shaking my head, I sucked my teeth then hesitantly discarded it into the nearby bushes. With my eyes closed, I released a sigh that was somehow loud enough to awaken them because just as I reopened my eyes, they all rose from the pavement. One after the other they took a defensive stance and greeted me with unfriendly grins of their canine teeth and throttled of growls with bristled hair that reminded me that I had just intruded on their territory. Panic set in for a moment, since I couldn't outrun them. With courage, and the concealment of my fears along with continuous eye contact, I hopped towards as they observed my every move and viciously barked at me simultaneously as if they wanted to launch an attack. Each hop I took toward them, their aggressive barks slowly turned into quiet whines with their tails wiggled and heads curiously dancing from side to side and their eyes fixed on me in a merciful, mutual gaze that left me completely astonished. Passing them didn't convince me that I was clear of an ambush, but the further I hopped away, their whines decreased. Just as I reached a safe distance, I looked back and saw that the same vicious dogs that attacked everyone who entered their territory stood in solidarity with their eyes glued onto me with wiggled tails as if to say, "Poor helpless thing. It's just a waste of our time to even bluff a charge at him."

The next day, my knee was huge and much stiffer. The pain made me flinch and pant to every move, and my knee couldn't extend past the 90-degree angle. My aunt's husband was unable to take me to the hospital, which meant that my only option was to hop down the hill and then onto the main road where I flagged the driver of a speeding minibus who looked at me and continued on for a moment before he came to a stop 20 feet from where I stood, aided on an actually cane. The conductor pushed his head out the window, and yelled, "Come, come," to which I first hesitated. I had expected the driver to have some form of sympathy toward me and reverse. As I hopped toward the vehicle, he shouted, "Man, you're taking too long like an old man" and drove off. His behavior didn't surprise me since many considered him to be one of the biggest idiots on the island. Fortunately, soon after, I was picked up by a friend who took me directly to the hospital.

DOMESTIC DETENTION

A few hours later, I returned home with my knee wrapped in a bandage, then sprawled myself on the grass inside of the yard as I stared toward the sky in a daze. Suddenly, I was distracted by the distant sound of an aircraft engine. It sounded much different from the ones that passed each day, and it appeared to be much bigger and was at a higher altitude. As it disappeared and reappeared from time to time through patches of white, scattered clouds before it went out of sight, everything about my mother's final hours at the airport flashed before my eyes. Something inside of me changed at that moment. I limped back inside the house and stood before the window, and stared at the swift moving traffic on the street that was about 150 meters away. Then everything–from the squeaked opened door I heard over the telephone, my mother's husband's dominant tone, the changed telephone numbers, and the unopened, returned letters–all bombarded my brain. Tears streamed down my cheeks. I made my way inside the bedroom and reached for the rejection letter taped to the mirror, stared at it for a moment, then knew that it was time for me to try a second time.

As my knee slowly healed, I secretly orchestrated my plan by jotting everything down on a piece of paper. My first plan was to get a simple, temporary job where I needed just enough money to purchase a return airline ticket for myself and one for my mother if needed. Luck struck a week later when someone informed me that help was needed at a nearby cafeteria owned by a well-known European, Vincentian family that also ran a housekeeping business on the same property. Soon after I was hired, and immediately noticed they had no regard for employees based on the verbal abuse that came from the daughter who burst out in anger uncontrollably on employees from time to time. It didn't take long for me to experience the same verbal abuse. We were walking towards each other when she smiled at me, and I said "good morning" with a smile on my face. She responded, but I honestly thought that she had replied "good morning" and I kept on moving. Suddenly, she burst out,"I'm talking to you. How dare you walk away from me when I'm talking to you?" Shocked by her outburst, I released a loud sigh to calm myself now to prevent a migraine, then listened as she babbled on, then off the bat I checked her, and let her know that neither my mother, father, aunts or uncles had ever spoken to me in such a manner, and demanded that she never speak to me in such tone ever again. Ever since I was young, I'd alway believed that a person should speak to you nicely about something first, and if it's repeated numerous times, then I can understand the outburst, but to burst out like that made me realize how angry she was. Later that day she apologized, but it didn't appear genuine. My observation also convinced me that neither she nor her mother was trustworthy of us employees based on my first encounter with the mother when I decided to assist a coworker who had already worked six consecutive hours on his feet and needed a break. The head chef was busy and asked him to prepare numerous sandwiches, and since I had limited work, I quickly volunteered. "I'll do it," I said. "You sure?" the coworker asked. "Yeah, man. You've been working all day," I replied. As he made his exit, I unwrapped a sliced loaf of bread, cut each corner, discarded all the crust inside the trash, then made the sandwiches. After everything was completed, the mother entered, looked at the sandwiches, and asked, "You made these?" I replied, "Yeah." She abruptly continued, "And you didn't take any?" Shocked by the question, I was startled and responded, "No." In a manner that I considered to be out of line, she asked, "Are you sure about that?" As much as I wanted to explode, I knew I needed the money to purchase my airline ticket, plus I didn't want to trigger my migraine, so I contained myself and responded, "No, I didn't" in the calmest tone possible. With her unwashed hands, she began to fit every slice of bread together like a puzzle, then counted them all and noticed that they were all accounted for. Instead of apologizing, she exited the kitchen without saying a word. As much as I was tempted to demand an apology, I shook my head and forgot about everything. I realized that I was only there for a short time and decided that it was best to remain quiet, but what I learnt,that day, was that people only respect you based on your level of position, and those who never apologize for any wrongdoings think very little of you. From that moment on, she was placed in my black book, which is a list of people that I needed to keep my eyes on or to avoid.

After what took place, the head chef–who was a very big man, about 6'4", 220 pounds– approached me and apologized. From that day on, we began to talk a lot and he'd always asked about my parents. I found it kind of odd, but only mentioned that my mother was away and never went into any details, but he somehow sensed that my father was also not on the island. The more we chatted, I began to notice that there was something sinister about him. He was a man who appeared from out of nowhere and not many people in the area knew much about him, except that he was a chef. Whenever he was teaching me how to prepare new dishes, he stood very close to me, which made me very uncomfortable. There were times when I saw him through the reflection door of the refrigerator with both hands on his hips staring at me as if it was normal.

Whenever I asked "Is something wrong?" he responded by saying, "Just thinking, that's all." To me, that type of behavior was strange, and it didn't take long for his true intention to come out when one evening I left the workplace early and had to return for something that I had forgotten. Where I lived was only a five-minute walk away, and I quickly slipped into a sleeveless T-shirt, raced back to the workplace, and grabbed what I needed. On my way out, I encountered him and with a fake smile, he said, "You're exposing skin, man." As much as I didn't trust him, his comment never registered since it could have been interpreted in several different ways such as, "This is a place of business, you can't be in here wearing a sleeveless shirt" or, "Shouldn't you be covered up since you're that skinny?" This was the Caribbean and sleeveless tops are often worn by many, so I didn't think much of the comment. The following day on my way out, he asked, "What are you doing later?" "Nothing," I replied, thinking nothing of it. "You're always free after work?" he continued to ask. I was never the type of person to ask anyone "Why" after being asked a question, but I began to figure that he was getting at something. Curious about what it was, I asked, "Why?" "You seem to be very interested in how a lot of the dishes are made, so I wouldn't mind showing you how to make several more," he said. "Oh, thanks, then we can do that tomorrow?" I said. "No, I was thinking more of you coming over to my place tonight since the ovens here are always occupied." His comment concerned me, and I began to realize that he was attempting to lure me over to his house. Feeling uneasy, my blood gushed to my head, but I quickly calmed myself down whileI hid my discomfort. On the other hand, I thought of how fair it would be to prove whether or not he was guilty or innocent, so I quietly replied, "Give me a bit to think about it," even though I knew that there wasn't a chance that I was going to show up to his house alone. I got home that evening and had completely forgotten about the conversation when at 8 p.m., the phone rang. I answered, and the first words that came out of the caller's mouth were, "Don't forget to come, but alone." "Huh?" I said as it took a moment for everything to register inside my head before I realized that it was him. My blood ran cold, and I said, "Just show me when I come in to work tomorrow. I mean, I can always stand and watch you prepare whatever." "It's going to be too busy," he responded. "Then we can always do it another day," I said, but he still wasn't taking "No" for an answer. Concerned that his persistence would only prolong and irritate the living daylights out of me, I finally said "Yes." He reminded me that I needed to come alone. "Sure," I replied, hung the phone up, then raced over to my neighbor who I'll call "Brinks" and informed him about what was happening. Brinks quickly rounded up another person who I'll call "stalk" who agreed to come along for extra protection then. The funny thing was that Brinks was the shortest, about 4 feet 11 inches, and Stalk who was about my height, about 5 feet 11 inches at the time, wasn't much bigger than I was. We were both slim built. and was in no match for a man 6ft and over two hundred pounds. We were young and adventurous, and needed to see what the chef was up to. Like a celebrity protected by my two bodyguards who were both unarmed, we headed out under the brilliant moonlight with absolutely no fear, giggled as we pumped fists and laughed our way until we got to the house which was barely lit. Not sure if it was due to the brilliant moonlight or because he was expecting me. The entire living room was completely dark.

The strategy was to have one person positioned at the entrance and the other at the back of the house. If I found myself in any danger, I was to flick a light switch off and on or, if I wasn't out of the house by a certain time, then Brinks was to first rush in for the rescue, followed by Stalk. There wasn't supposed to be any form of violence unless I was attacked and needed to defend myself.

Just as we got to the house, Stalk made his way toward the back of the house and we watched his silhouette disappear. Then for quick concealment, Brinks darted like an infantry into some nearby bushes and couldn't even be recognized under the glittered moonlight.

I approached the house, softly knocked on the sliding, glass door, and within an instant, the curtain slid to one side and revealed the silhouette of the chef towered behind the door. His body stood like a giant sequoia. His arms built like two massive posts, and were barely visible under the cover of darkness. Instantly, I realized his intention. I panicked, and became very much uncomfortable and wanted to take off running, but we wanted enough proof to see whether or not there was an undercover predator who was walking the streets of our neighborhood, preying on young boys or girls. Suddenly a button on the door clicked, then the door slid open on one side just wide enough for me to slip my narrow frame through as he asked, "Alone?", I nodded "Yes," then he removed himself from the doorway as an indication for me to enter, but I hesitated. "Let me take my shoes off. You can turn the living room light on in the meantime" I said. As he did, I scanned the entire living room until my eyes met every available light switch, then I hesitantly entered the house. "Lock the door," he said before he made his way into the back.

I took the opportunity and signaled Brinks with a thumb's up to make sure he was still in position and heard him respond with a quiet whistle that was loud enough for me to hear.

In order to convince the chef that I had locked the door, I moved away from the side of the door where I entered, made my way toward the side of the door that was locked, and unlocked that side. It produced a loud click that convinced the chef that I had locked the side of the door where I entered, when in fact, both sides of the door were left unlocked. If a quick escape was ever needed, I would have then escaped through the side of the door that he thought was locked.

My heart pounded as I made my way down the corridor. The light decreases with each step I made away from the living room. "What if security number one and two decided to run off, and left me alone to defend myself against a 6'4, 220-pound, hefty man who had the strength of a Gorilla. My heart pounded harder and harder until I got to the doorway of the bedroom where my eyes met a bottle of liquor that stood between two empty glasses, and a sealed pack of condoms beside them under a dull, lit night lamp. I stopped. Just then, from the corner of my eye, I saw the silhouette of Stalk snaking around the toilet ventilation pole like a go-go dancer with his index finger sealed over his lips in a silent gesture that indicated to me that he was on guard. After quickly looking away to avoid suspension, I thought of how sick, and disgusted the chef was. The liquor and condoms were obvious signs of his intention, but like three detectives, we still needed solid proof through a confession. I pointed toward the sealed pack of condoms then asked, "What's that for?" He couldn't even look at me. The guilt appeared on his face, then after a moment, he stated his intention. After about five minutes of talking, Brink appeared behind me. "You cool?" he asked, and I replied, "Yeah, man." The chef widened his eyes in shock, his face dropped, then he sighed just before he hung his head in shame. Without saying a word, I shook my head, then made my exit, and left behind. On my way out, Stalk entered.

Seated along in the veranda, I thought about how dangerous this man was, and wondered if he had ever seduced any underage person to his house. After a moment, Brinks and Stalk exited the house with bottles of liquor in hand and stated that the chef confessed about his secret lifestyle, which we never cared about. It wasn't our business, and he was free to live his life and do whatever he pleased. Exposing him was never our intention. I was 18 years of age, Stalk was 17, and Brinks was 19. We all made the chef a promise that we'd keep his lifestyle a secret. In return, he was to abide by the law, and was never to lure anyone under the age of 16 over to his house whether it was a male or female.

As much as his behavior affected me, my friends and I still find time to talk and laugh about it whenever we get the chance. To this day, the chef's identity and lifestyle remain a secret to us and will continue to remain that way unless he decides to come out on his own.

The next day, after collecting my income, the chef pulled me aside and calmly asked in an upset manner, "What was that all about last night?" "Are you serious?", I asked, "That was very childish of you," he continued, and that caused me to shoot back at him, "Well, maybe it's because I'm a child who you tried to seduce. You're a sick man," but he never responded. I continued. "You're a predator who lured me over with the intention of getting me drunk to advantage me," but he still didn't respond "Are you aware of the danger you could be in if we mention this to anyone?" I asked, and he still didn't respond. "My friends and I decided to put this all behind us and leave you alone to live your life because we don't care, and you're coming to me with this crap. Are you serious, man?" We stared at each other for a moment as he bobbed his head, then in a calm tone, said, "I'll put a Haitian voodoo priest on you." "Am I supposed to be scared?", I asked. "You should be," he replied, then I burst out laughing while shaking my head. "So the same person who was forgiven now decides to put a voodoo priest on the person who forgave him?" I asked, but he never replied; I continued, "Listen, whatever you do is your business. Feel free to live your life, but to invite me to your house for the sole purpose of getting me drunk so you could take advantage of me has to be the sickest thing I have ever experienced, and I'm not saying this because I'm a male. It's nothing different from a man luring a female into his home. It's just that the overall intention makes me sick." Then in a calm but angry tone he shot back, "But you didn't have to say anything to anyone." I looked at him with a calm demeanor, then said, "You have to be a fool to think that I would be stupid enough to come to your house alone, especially at night. I wouldn't even be this stupid to enter a female's house unless I know for a fact that she's single." I shook my head in disgust before asking for my money. He reached for an envelope and handed it to me. "Thank you," I said, then headed toward the exit where I stopped and looked at him one final time, then said, "Get your Haitian voodoo priest," and with that, made my exit.

CHAPTER FIVE:
THE ARRANGEMENT

NOT HAVING ENOUGH RESOURCES FOR MY MOTHER'S RESCUE mission made me reach out to my aunts and one uncle who never hesitated to assist me in any way. Within a few weeks, all of my documents were gathered, and I made sure that I wasn't short of anything listed on the application to avoid a second rejection. Everyone was still in the dark about my plan, and I wanted it to remain that way until I found the closure that was very much needed,

To everyone, it was a normal trip like everyone else who mainly travels to North America during their vacation, and since it was planned for the winter, many assumed that I wanted to experience the snow.

A few weeks later, I was high-spirited on an island not too far from St. Vincent, crammed inside of a minibus, and wasn't even bothered by the fidgeted passenger seated beside me, who probably did her very best to irritate me. Ten minutes later, I found myself in the city, totally confused as I scanned my surroundings like an uncontrollable, rotating water hose. "You look lost," a female street vendor said. "Not really, I'm just looking for the embassy," I said. "Well, which means, you're lost," she continued with a giggle. "Go all the way down and make a right," she said. I replied "Thank you." I raced off through the crowded street and got to the building within five minutes. It was evident due to the building's vacancy that I was at the wrong location. A second lady who walked by saw that I was looking confused and said, "If you're looking for the embassy, it moved but I have no idea where to." "Thank you," I replied. I sighed and shook my head. Frustrated that my time had run out, I continued on until a few people redirected me back to the previous building that was vacant. "You have to be joking, I said to myself. I decided to approach a man who said, "You need to hop back onto a minibus because they moved to a new building and it will take you a while to get there on foot." For a minute, I stopped to consider. "What if he's also wrong?I'd be much further away and that could cause a longer delay", I said to myself. After a moment of thinking, I took his advice, and hopped back onto a minibus, and within a few minutes, I got to the correct building and immediately joined a fast moving line, and handed my passport over to a woman seated inside a booth detached from the main building. My eyes were fixed on her as she scrutinized it before handing it back over to me. I then made my way through a glass door where a security guard instructed me to take off my belt and empty my pockets into a container. "Any weapons?" he asked as he passed the wand over my entire body. "No sir," I said, but for the fun of it, I was very much tempted to respond

"Yes", but didn't since I realized that such a joke would have most likely jeopardized my mission. I proceeded into a large, crowded room where many stood in silence. Some sucked their teeth in disappointment as others walked away in tears after being denied by two women with solemn faces, seated at separated windows behind two glass walls. Seated beside them was a younger gentleman who appeared quite modest and was in full focus, carefully organizing a pile of papers.

More than an hour had passed before the line finally dwindled to a man ahead of me who shook his head, fidgeted, sighed from time to time, and used curse words loudly enough that only me could have heard. His frustration came from nervousness as he explained to me the number of times he was denied. "Could you believe I was denied three times?" he turned to me and said. His comment bothered me, and I did my best to avoid the conversation out of fear that answering him may have caused him to say something negative that may have affected me. His body language was quite lame, and his posture indicated a man lacking communication skills. To think that he was prepared for an interview made me guess, but it didn't take long for everything to be revealed. Just as the lady behind the glass wall signaled him toward her, he sighed. I watched him shake his head in disappointment and asked myself, "Why would he do such a thing while the lady was looking at him? He took one step forward and lost his footing, then stumbled to the ground like a slab of wood as all eyes turned toward him. "Are you ok?" several asked, but instead of responding, he picked himself up and strolled toward the window with his head hung like a lame duck before sliding the documents under the glass partition with his trembled hands. My eyes were still stuck on him as he glanced away from time to time during his questioning, and leant forward against the counter as he shook his head before slipping both hands inside his pants pocket. In my opinion, he was already asking to be rejected for a fourth time.

Soon after, a female applicant walked away from the window beside him. She too had her head hung to the floor, which to me was proof that she was denied. The lady behind the window then looked at me and as our eyes met, a tremor of anxiety instantly intimidated me, but I avoided the obvious by simply looking away. "Looks like you're next," the lady behind me said in her unique island accent, and without looking at her, I replied, "I guess," with my shoulders shrugged. With my heart pounding through my shirt, I took a quick glance at the lady behind the window, only to see her glanced back at me as she adjusted her seat before stacking a pile of paper. The anxiety caused by her quick glance made my heart pound faster and louder, and to calm myself, I looked away and stared at the floor in a daze, and was expecting her to call me at any moment. For some unknown reason, I lifted my head and looked toward the window, and the gentleman who was seated beside her, signaled me toward him. It was as if I was physically ushered toward him by the hand of God. I closed my eyes and sighed a loud relief, then walked toward him, then as I did, the woman beside him signaled the lady behind to walk toward her. "Cheese on bread," she burst out of frustration, which is "Wow!" for her island slang. As much as I felt her frustration, I had no choice but to thank God that He had spared me.

As I walked toward the counter, I realized that the hardest part of my mission hadn't even yet started, but with confident, I handed my documents over to the gentleman and greeted him by saying "Good morning, Sir," then watched as he meticulously scanned through every piece of documentation from behind the thick lens of his glasses. After a moment, he lifted his head, stared me in my eyes, and began to question me. To every question asked, I replied truthfully with confidence, and not once did I glance away from him. As he continued to look through my documents, I glanced at the lady who stood in line behind me, but was now standing beside me and saw that her fingers were trembling nervously on the counter like a virtuoso pianist running their fingers across the piano keys. I looked toward her feet in search of bodily waste, but it appeared that she was fortunate enough to control her bladder. All of a sudden, I thought I'd heard a faint voice say, "Check the window outside at 1 p.m.," but I wasn't sure since all my attention was on the lady. It wasn't until a second time when I heard the voice say "Sir!" that I realized it was the gentleman. I quickly switched my attention back toward him. "Pardon me," I said, and he replied. "I said to check the outside window at 1 p.m." He handed me a ticket, and as I took it, I realized that one hurdle was completed. I closed my eyes and breathed a sigh of relief, then calmly exited the building.

Two hours later, I collected my documentation and passport from the window at the outside booth, and without even looking at it, I returned to the guest house where I stayed, and the first thing I did was fall on my knees and thanked God for clearing hurdle number one.

The following morning, I awoke to dazzling sunlight on a day that was too beautiful to resist the outdoors. I entered a nearby restaurant where a young lady was drooped behind a cash register with her arms folded and her thoughts miles away. "Good morning," I said with a smile, and she politely replied, "Good morning" in a South American accent. Her body language revealed a depressed young lady and even though I'm never the one to start a conversation, I somehow decided to keep going in an attempt to cheer her up. "You're not a morning person, are you?", I said. "Not really. It's just the same old every day, but you can only hope things will get better" she replied. "Oh! You bet it will. It's only a matter of time.", I said before reaching for a soft drink from the refrigerator then placed it on the counter in front of her. Her South American accent was a big giveaway, but I still needed the conversation to keep going, and asked "Where are you from?" She smiled before giving the name of the South American country which I had already guessed correctly. With a smiling face, she continued, "I guess we can't hide. You're from St. Vincent, right?" "Yeah, but I'm leaving tonight," I said. She quietly looked toward the floor in a depressed mood that for some reason became my concern. For a minute, I thought of taking the drink back to the guest house, then asked myself, "What if she just needed someone to talk to?" I struck a simple conversation up, then as it went on, she slowly opened up and informed me that her mother had migrated to New York, and left her behind at the age of 16. She met a man who was on a visit who she thought was single but was married. After getting pregnant by him, he returned to his wife. Soon after, her mother got the shocking news and abandoned her. Life became rough for her and she had no choice but to migrate, and left her four-year-old daughter behind.

I felt pity toward her. The way I saw it, she was just a young girl taken advantage of by a man who saw that she was vulnerable.

"How often do you speak with your daughter?" I asked. She became emotional, then sighed before she shook her head. "It's been over two months," she said as she swiped her fingers across her watery eyes without looking at me. I closed my eyes for a minute and imagined how painful it must have been for her and her daughter since she happened to be a young mother who didn't appear to be much older than 20. "Sorry if I seem a bit out of focus, but it's not easy living like this every day," she continued, and I replied, "It's ok, I understand." She handed me a photograph of her daughter who was a beautiful Dougla girl with brown, shiny eyes, and black, lengthy hair just below her shoulders. The more I looked at the child, the more I pitied them and decided to invite her over to where I was staying so that they could have spoken to each other over the telephone. Without hesitation, it was an offer she quickly accepted.

I left the store trying to figure out the mentality of parents who abandon their teenage daughters all because of a pregnancy, which for most of the time is nothing more than a mistake. It was something I saw a lot of growing up and to me, it never solved any problem. Neither does it make any sense. In my opinion, forcing a teenage girl to marry the man who impregnated her or abandoning her because of a pregnancy may only lead to multiple pregnancies.

At 2 p.m., she knocked on the door before she entered with a smiling face. After chatting for a bit, I pointed the phone out to her, then made my way inside the bedroom, and left her behind so she could have her privacy. Five minutes later, I heard sobbing and exited the room. Without saying a word, she hugged me and as I hugged her back, I felt her warm tears soak my T-shirt. I was taken over by emotion and began to realize that I too had missed out on almost 13 years of not having my mother around. Her laughter and the frequent trips she made every chance she got from her job at a nearby island before she migrated all flashed before me as the tears streamed from my eyes, and I quietly shook my head, knowing that I was one step closer to reuniting with her.

A moment went by before I broke the hug, and as I watched her make her way toward the chair, I saw an innocent girl who needed help at that point, I began to secretly orchestrate a reconciliation between her and her mother, but first, asked myself if I was willing to take on another challenge when I hadn't even begun the first.

After reconsidering for a moment with my arms folded, I asked "What's your mother's address?" She looked at me curiously, then said, "I have one from a long time ago, but not sure if she still lives there, why?" "I'll be going to New York in a few months, and I wouldn't mind trying to see if I can get in touch with her", I replied. At that moment, she didn't display any emotion, and neither was she elated in any way. Instead, she looked away, and I continued, "When was the last time you contacted her?" to which she replied, "Not since she found out that I was pregnant." I continued, "Then maybe, there's a chance that she tried contacting you, but you had already come here." "My cousins would have told me," she said. I paused for a moment, sighed, found a seat beside her, and continued in a soft tone, "It's never that easy for a person to come back and apologize to you after knowing that they have done you wrong. Sometimes, it's much easier for them to just stay away." "She's not like that," she said, then I replied, "I'm a male, but I can tell you for sure that it's always hard for a mother to walk away from a child after carrying her for nine months," but she never responded. Instead, she thought about it for a few seconds, then without saying another word, jotted her mother's address onto a piece of paper and handed it to me. I jokingly asked, "How about your number just in case I found her and wanted to inform you?" She burst out laughing, and displayed her sparkling white teeth as two dimples appeared on her cheeks. "Wow, this girl is really beautiful," I thought, then she asked, "Are you sure that's the reason for you asking?" I then burst out laughing, and replied, "Well, who knows where it can go from here." She shook her head as we both continued laughing before she wrote the telephone number onto a separate piece of paper, handed it to me, then said "Call before 7:00 p.m. because the lady I'm living with doesn't like late calls." I replied "Sure," then placed the paper inside of my bags.

All of a sudden, something commanded me to look through the window, and what I saw was the clear, blue skies, slowly transforming into a menacing shade of black clouds which concerned me for a bit. Not that I was afraid of flying in that type of weather, but in the event of a disaster, nothing beats being at home.

After dropping the young lady off, it was chaos as we pulled into the airport. All aircraft were at a standstill on the tarmac, and were barely visible through their outlines and pulsing lights. The runway and VASI lights faintly loomed in the background, and all airport staff who were outdoors had their HI-VIS. Sadly, frustrated passengers vented their anger on airport staff who had no control over the weather.

After a three-hour delay, we finally took off through the weather and were immediately swallowed by a blanket of fog. Everything reminded me of the incident of LIAT flight #319, which disappeared between St. Vincent and St. Lucia on a similar evening. That Sunday was a day like no other. As young teenagers, we were all taking part in a football match at the Calliaqua playing field when suddenly, the sunny evening skies were disrupted by a black blanket of clouds which extended beyond the horizon. Within minutes, daylight completely vanished. In an instant, a light rain commenced then intensified into a brutal, torrential sheet of downpour that battered our bodies like cairns of heavy pebbles. Thunder constantly rumbled as veins of lightning cracked through the open skies, and illuminated it like billions of fluorescent bulbs. Citizens were asked to remain in doors. As we sprinted off the field and into the pavilion, in the blink of an eye, the green, murky water from the river behind overflowed and surrounded us. As a group of young teenagers with no driver's license, our only way to escape the calamity was to venture back out into the hazardous conditions through partly submerged streets where water cascaded from a nearby downhill as thunder rumbled and lightning flashed above us. The following morning, we awoke to the sad news that several people including dignitaries, a former beauty contestant with a cheerful smile, and a man who lived 200 meters away from my house who was confined to a wheelchair for his entire life, all perished in an aircraft that went missing. This was a very polite man of distinction, a master at repairing watches among other skills, who never complained about his disadvantage. Neither did he allow it to slow him down. He was loved by everyone but what struck me most was to look across toward his house, and imagine seeing him struggling to stay afloat through treacherous waters, was something I couldn't bear to think about. For days, ships and aircraft searched the ocean for debris but the only thing found were specks of floating oil. Weeks after, a memorial service was held and a flag was hoisted in memory of them all.

CHAPTER SIX: THE MISSION

CHRISTMAS WAS JUST A FEW MONTHS AWAY AND IN PREPARAtion for my mission, everything remained a secret out of fear of being characterized as a man with psychosis disorder by anyone who was blind to my determination. I didn't want to be bombarded with questions such as "How are you going to find a woman who you don't have an address or a telephone number for?" or "How do you know that she's still alive?" They would have been questions that irritated me, but to give up on a woman who gave my sister and me her all didn't sit well at all with me.

Months went by, then on that December day of my departure, I prayed, then stared at a few photographs of her, then became emotional, but managed to hold back my tears. After I tucked one of the photos between the pages of my passport and the other inside one pant pocket, I reached for a paper with all of her previous addresses, and tucked it inside of my traveling bag. I then exited the house as I pulled the suitcase with one hand, and my other firmly holding the bag over my shoulder, and stepped out beneath the splendid sunlight where everything appeared still and quiet with all of my focus set on my mother.

I was completely muted and in a daze as I silently stared out the window with the breeze of the moving vehicle hitting my face while I was unable to think straight. I pondered the outcome and began to wonder if it was something that I was ready to accept, but all I had was to complete one job and that was to find my mother at any cost. There was no time for shopping, sightseeing, or even meeting anyone I hadn't seen in ages. It was as if I was in a state of oblivion in another world where everything was quiet, yet no one understood me. The plan was for me to spend the time granted while I kept in touch with the FBI, and if by the end of my mission she wasn't found, then I was to return home and try again at a certain time. I had no intention of ever giving up until I got the closure everyone needed.

After I checked it at the airport, I then made my way toward the waiting area, and stopped. Everything about my mother's final moment before she boarded the aircraft flashed before my eyes. It was as if she stood there and was wiping her teary eyes before she disappeared inside of the room. It wasn't until someone asked me repeatedly to excuse them that I realized I was having a flashback.

The waiting room was quiet when I entered. After being seated, I folded my arms and vaguely gazed at the floor and wasn't even mindful of all the murmuring and chattering around me. My mind was on my mother, reminiscing on the days my sister and I spent with her, then I was overcome by a sudden emotion that caused me to somehow smile.

After an unexpectedly short wait, boarding was announced. I reached for my bag from the seat beside me, and felt a perception of nervousness and took a deep breath before shaking my head. For a moment, I wondered if it was all a dream. As I took my seat on the aircraft, with my eyes closed, I released a sigh before shaking my head on what was the beginning of a desperate journey of uncertainty.

Hours into the flight after nibbling on a bite-size piece of fish and a couple of spoonfuls of rice that couldn't even satisfy my baby-size stomach, my knee began to hurt after I unconsciously kept it in a bent position for an extensive amount of time. It was stiff and swollen and felt as though it stuck onto my pants much tighter than spandex. The slightest movement caused it pain, which concerned me after reading somewhere that excessive flying can cause blood clots. Fearing that the worst could happen, I signaled to the flight attendant who immediately came to my assistance. "My leg is a bit swollen, is it possible for me to walk around the aisle for a bit?" I asked, but she politely said that I couldn't, then instructed me to fasten my seatbelt in preparation for landing.

In less than a minute, the muffling sound of the whistling aircraft engine grew louder. A ping was heard over the intercom followed by the quiet voice of the same flight attendant, "Ladies and gentlemen, please make sure that your seatbelts are securely fastened for landing." I positioned myself as the engines revved before it thrusted us out of the thick, gray plume of clouds. Suddenly, we emerged into the void of darkness. I wiped the frosted window with the palm of my hand and peered out through obscured vision onto New York

City. It appeared beneath us in a canopy of white spanned by bridges and congested highways, punctuated by dots of lights from slow-moving vehicles and buildings that appeared like islands in a foggy ocean. The reality of the mission in the city that many say never sleeps suddenly hit me with fear. I somehow found myself buried by anhedonia but quietly kept it all together, knowing that the closure I was so desperate to find may not have been the one I was prepared to accept.

As the aircraft came to a stop, passengers ripped their seat belts off before they sprung to their feet and scavenged through the overhead compartment like a bunch of looters tearing a clothing store apart. I, on the other hand, patiently remained seated like a mannered young man. After the aisle was cleared, I pulled my bag from the overhead compartment, flung my sweater over my shoulder, and exited the aircraft. I got to the arrival area and joined a long line of passengers, snaked around the room until I was called by a female immigration officer who I calmly approached, and laid my passport before her, knowing that she was the only obstacle who could have prevented me from beginning my mission. "Good night.", I said. "Good night, Sir," she responded politely as she flipped through the pages of my passport before stopping with her eyes fixed on the photograph of my mother. I had forgotten to remove it, but never expected it to cause any issue. Something about the photograph interested her. She asked "Your mother? You look a lot like her." I nodded "yes", then she continued, "Visiting her?" I became speechless and couldn't respond for a moment since I wasn't sure if I'd get to see her before my time expired. After a short moment, I replied, "I don't know where she is." The officer paused for a moment, staring at me, then continued, "You look a lot younger than your age." "I get that all the time," I replied. After all of my questions were answered truthfully, she handed my passport back to me, and just like that, my biggest hurdle was cleared. I sighed with my head shaking, then slipped into my sweater, grabbed my suitcases, and headed toward the customs area only to have every fruit that I walked with taken away. That was the least of my worries. Another huddle was cleared, and that was my only concern.

As I exited the airport, the reality that I was closer than ever to finding closure overcame me. I stopped for a moment, closed my eyes, then after the release of a loud sigh, I exited the airport, and was hit by a blast of wet, arctic air that struck me like a shock wave. For the first time, I thought to myself how quickly a difference in location can make. Five hours before, I was only wearing a T-shirt. In a short space of time, it was as if I was trapped inside an expansive deep freeze.

The next day, I crawled out of bed, slid the curtain, and peered out into a hazy morning. My eyes fixed on a brown, barren tree just a few feet away from behind the closed, glass window, curious about its species. A scan of the surroundings, squinting through a smog of fog instantly left me in a depressed mood and caused me to move away from the window and switch from radio station to radio station in search of Christmas carols. It was to no avail. The television weather report had me completely confused before I realized that the temperature was on the Fahrenheit scale. My slight memory of a conversion was to subtract 32 from a number, then multiplying that number by .5556, which almost caused my brain to explode. Instead, my easiest solution was to crack the window open just enough to pierce my hand into the cold air and determine whether it was too cold enough for me to bear.

Out of the blue, the face of a missing woman along with the phrase "Have you seen this person?" appeared on the television screen. The idea of me reaching out to the station crossed my mind, but the length of time in which the woman's face was shown on the television was only about five seconds. To me, that wasn't long enough for anyone to recognize her. I considered contacting a program such as "Unsolved Mysteries," but I was very much afraid that doing so meant that there was a possibility of my mother's husband seeing her face on television, which could have caused him to go deeper into hiding. Quickly, I changed my mind and decided that it was best to remain with my original plan, which was to contact the FBI.

For the next two days, the cold, gloomy forecast had me under house arrest, and depressed, and I figured it was time for me to venture into the cold. After cracking the window open, I felt the temperature was bearable, then I slipped into an oversized coat, exited the apartment, then made my way down the sidewalk where a middle-aged man in a sweater three times his size dressed in a pair of pants, sagged from his waist, and an untied pair of boots approached me. "Got any money?" he asked. "I ain't ha "nutten," I said in my thick Caribbean accent. "So, you're telling me that you don't even have a dollar?" he continued. As much as I found his question to be quite bold, I wasn't sure if he was armed, so I fiddled with my pocket to show him that it was pretty much empty, then watched as he moved away with one of the weirdest, distinctive walks I had ever seen. With one hand grabbed at the front of his pants to prevent it from falling, he stepped out with his feet dragged onto the ground as he bobbed his head and rocked both shoulders from side to side. As much as I wanted to burst out laughing, I smiled, then shook my head.

My stroll took me onto Nostrand Avenue, a familiar place many spoke about. According to them, a certain area had a reputation that I soon came to realize, after I saw a man arguing with two police officers who quietly stood outside their vehicle. The man carried on with the most "F" notes I had ever heard, and I was curious as to why he wasn't arrested. Using such a word on most Caribbean Islands will surely land you in a cell plus a fine. I later came to find out that such a word is accepted on U.S. soil.

The following Sunday after exiting church, I took notice of several police vehicles parked outside of a precinct, and wanted to approach, but I was surrounded by relatives, and wasn't yet ready to disclose any information about my mission. A few days into the new year, everything was getting to me. I desperately wanted to visit the precinct, but I was very much concerned that the officers there may have still been in the high holiday spirit and may be a bit inattentive toward my plea. That idea was quickly squashed and since the internet was still in its infancy, I reached for the yellow pages in search of the FBI, and hoped that I'd get the opportunity to speak to a female agent who would probably look at everything from a female's perspective and understand what my mother was going through. At the last second, a light bulb lit up inside my head. The times I called my mother and heard the message "sorry, the number you called has been changed"crossed my mind. "What if I can dial a very old number that she once had, while she was living in New York City, and that number leads me onto a different number that I can track.?" I asked myself. At the time, the idea sounded crazy, and I was very much skeptical, but what if it worked, I continued to ask myself. After closing the yellow pages, I got to my feet, paced the floor restlessly until my aunt's husband returned from work. I allowed him to relax and play the piano as he normally did as I glanced at the clock on the wall, and patiently waited for him to take a break. When he finally did, I asked, "Do you have any old New York telephone numbers for my mother?" He paused for a moment and looked at me in shock, then said "I have an old number, but remember, that was from a very long time ago. Did she contact you or something?" "Just wanted to see if I can find her," I replied. In the back of my head, I feared that being questioned too much might have led to me having negative thoughts about finding her.

Everything was halted for a few more days, then one day he approached the telephone with an old book in hand filled with numbers and addresses. It was twisted and worn with loose pages that were somewhat tainted yellow with age. Watching him quietly turned the pages before reaching for the telephone made my heart pound against my chest. I became dizzy out of nervousness, but my migraine wasn't triggered. As he dialed the number, I sighed in silent discomfort as he placed the receiver to his ear. Expecting to hear him say, "hello" at any minute, he turned to me instead, then said, "It seems as though this number has changed, but it led me to another number so, I'm gonna dial this one." Suddenly, my heart skipped a beat. It was exactly what I wanted to hear, and figured the more numbers we dialed could lead us to her current number. He dialed a second number and my heart pounded for a second time, only to then be disappointed after he was greeted with the same message, which led to him dialing a third number. The dialing continued for some time as if it was a standard routine, then finally I heard him say, "Hello" and then call my mother's name. My eyebrows rose in astonishment, and my heart thudded against my shirt as he began to converse with the person on the other line. I wasn't sure who the person was, and tried my best to eavesdrop, but couldn't hear a thing from the person on the other end of the phone. Finally, I was handed the phone. My blood immediately gushed to my head, and felt as if it was about to explode. A migraine slightly triggered, and I quickly closed my eyes for a second. After releasing a puff of air, I took the receiver with a trembled hand, my knees quivered and I felt my heart beating profusely. In a cracked voice, I said "Hello," only to hear a woman with an American accent in a quiet, sympathetic voice reply, "Hi, how are you?" "Ok," I replied, as I began to wonder who she was. "It must be a very long time since you last saw your mom, huh?" she asked, and I replied, "Almost 14 years." She paused for a short moment, then in a sorrowful tone said, "I'm sorry to tell you, but your mother isn't doing too well." My eyes widened in shock, my heart dropped, and I became speechless. As much as I panicked, and felt sadly, I was still happy to know that she was still alive as I had predicted. I wanted to ask if she was my mother's caregiver or a friend, but decided not to out of fear that asking too many questions could lead me to lose contact once more. Instead, I asked, "Can I speak with my mother?" "She isn't here at the moment, but I'll have someone give you a call maybe today or tomorrow. Is that ok?" she asked. "Sure," I replied, then the conversation ended. I was very much convinced the person who was going to call would be my mother's husband and as much as I didn't want to hear his voice, I realized that he was my only way toward her.

 I wasted no time in relating my mother's condition to all of my relatives who were happy to know that she was alive, but sad to know that she wasn't doing too well. As I waited for the call that seemed like forever, I couldn't sleep that night. I tossed and turned restlessly, wondering if she was gravely ill somewhere on a hospital deathbed.

The following day, I walked my cousins to school, then raced back home and tried to calm myself down as I awaited the call. Nervous and happy at the same time, I couldn't sit. With the television volume turned down to the lowest, I paced the floor continuously, sighed with my head shaking from time to time, when suddenly the phone rang. My heart stopped. It took a few seconds for me to reach for the receiver with a shaking hand as a gush of blood shot through me like a bullet. Out of fear that a migraine could be triggered, I quickly calmed myself down, reached for the phone, then softly said "Hello." I was expecting to hear my mother's husband's voice but instead, I heard the cheerful voice of a woman with a southern American accent. It was like an electric jolt shot through my body as my heart pounded. My lips and body trembled, and I was left completely baffled as to who the person was. Not that I was concerned about the accent, but the person sounded quite upbeat. As she continued to speak, I began to ask myself if this was someone impersonating my mother and if her illness was exaggerated as a psychological attempt to make us believe that she was alive and doing well, when in fact, she was already dead or if it was a trap to lure me in. I just couldn't understand how a woman could be so ill for all those years and sound so cheerful. I wanted to ask a few questions to confirm that it was her, but out of concern that her husband was most likely listening in on the other end, I decided not to ask such questions. The call lasted no more than six minutes, but after it ended, I was left so bewildered that I couldn't even remember what the conversation was about. I wanted to inform my relatives that I wasn't too sure if the person I spoke with was my mother but decided not to. Reaching out fo the FBI was my second thing on my mind, but again, I was too afraid that if they intervened–and in fact the woman was my mother–then her husband would take off with her once again to an unknown place where we may never hear or see her again.

After purchasing a calling card the following day, I called her, hoping that I'd get the opportunity to speak to her privately. When I called, my four-year-old sister answered and passed the phone over to her. Since I wasn't sure how close she was seated to my mother, I kept the conversation normal. As we began to speak, I heard a completely different woman from who I spoke with the previous day. Even though the voice was the same. She was no longer the cheerful lady I spoke to the day before. She sounded dull and low, as if the world was on her shoulder. Still not sure who I was speaking with, I wanted to ask her several questions to make sure that it was her but decided to wait until we spoke about an upcoming reunion that made her emotional. I wasn't sure if they were tears of joy, sorrow, or for whatever unfortunate position she was in. The more we spoke, it was as if time was of the essence, and I became more desperate for a conclusion behind the entire mystery.

CHAPTER SEVEN: THE REUNION

After a little over a week of talking to my mother, it was time for me to visit and find out the truth about everything. In the back of my head, I was still skeptical that one of the voices heard during our conversation may not be hers and thought that it was probably a game to lure me in. I decided not to say anything to anyone in my family since I didn't want them to be worried about anything, but I confided in a close friend who had migrated for some time and knew about everything, from the time my mom went missing up to the point I spoke with her.

After hours of bursting my brain trying to figure out what my mother would look like, I strolled across to the corner store where I gathered a stack of candies for my four-year-old sister, then returned home. I couldn't concentrate that entire day. Not knowing any details about my mother's illness completely baffled me and led me to believe that since the cause of many women's deaths in the U.S. happen to be breast cancer, the thought that she was somewhere as a hospice patient lying on a hospital bed during her final days of stage-four cancer, crossed my mind and brought tears to my eyes.

I called my friend and related everything to her, then she began to sob. I quickly comforted her and assured her that I'd be ok, then gave her the number to the New York FBI's office with instructions to call if she hadn't heard from me by 10 a.m. the following day. Finally, that day came as everything flashed across my mind. Still not knowing what to expect, I glanced at my mother's photograph that was still tucked between the pages of my passport. Her impeccable smile, and her natural hair extended to top of her shoulders made me shake my head after realizing that she wasn't the same woman I'd expected to see in that physical condition. I paced the floor continuously as I shook my head in anger before finding a seat on the couch. After glancing at the clock, I finally got to my feet clad in a suit and tie like James Bond on a one man mission. I reached for my bag in the chair, and headed out, into the cold, wet, gloomy February morning, then stepped into the backseat of an awaiting taxi driven by a Haitian immigrant. He was friendly enough to strike up a conversation, but my dull response of "Yes" and "No" quickly caused him to stop talking. All I wanted was to be alone. I slipped the headset of my Walkman over my ear. It was the means of entertainment most people used apart from the cd player before 2007 when iPhone and iPod were non-existent. Increasingly feeling uncertain, the thought of a bitter-sweet reunion hypnotized me into a daze. Suddenly, a stentorian blast of "Groovy Kind of Love" by Phil Collins that the driver blared over the speaker, perhaps out of retaliation for my intentional disregard of him, brought me out of my trance.

A half-hour later, we pulled up to LaGuardia Airport swarmed by the heavy presence of armed military personnel due to the U.S. invasion of a Middle-Eastern country. I exited the taxi and headed for the check-in counter where I handed my passport over to a lady who flipped through the pages before asking "No other form of identification?" "No," I replied, then was given back my passport. As I made my way toward security, I removed the batteries from my walkman so that they would last much longer. Reaching the security, I emptied my entire pockets, placed everything including my walkman inside a container, then walked through the detector without any problems. It wasn't until I was cleared and had already walked about 50 feet away that a female shouted"Stop him!" I froze in my tracks and didn't even breathe, out of fear. For a moment, I thought that something illegal was found in my possession, my heart pounded as I froze in complete panic until the woman asked to check my Walkman to make sure that it was playable. After replacing the batteries inside of it, It was proved to be working, but not to their satisfaction as I watched them carefully inspect every component of it before handing it back over to me.

After breathing a sigh of relief, I proceeded into the passenger's waiting area and quietly crouched myself on a chair with my arms folded and my eyes staring blankly toward the floor with thoughts of whether the lady I spoke with was my mother or not. "If it is, has she gained weight or has she grown in any way?" I asked myself before pulling a piece of paper from my bag with several written questions that needed answers to. Each question appeared to be more like cross-examination that brought a cloud of guilt over me, and after realizing how loving and caring my mother was toward my sister and me and how much she never for once raised her voice at us or hit us in any way, my eyes became watery. I shredded the paper with my hand, then discarded it into the nearby trash bin.

With my watery eyes, I stepped onto the aircraft and was instantly noticed by a flight attendant who asked if I was ok, and I replied, "Yes," but her training and experience told her that I wasn't. Minutes after we took off, she sat beside me for a moment and as we began to chat, I opened up. She was quite happy to know that I was finally getting the chance to see my mother after so many years and wished me nothing but the very best.

Hours into our final descent, reality finally hit me and everything flashed across my mind–the numerous phone calls made from St. Vincent, the countless sleepless nights, the trip for my visa, and the uncertainty of the person I spoke with on the phone, all flashed across my mind and caused me to bury my face in the palm of my hands before I took the time to pull myself together.

Moments later after making my way across the jet bridge, I emerged inside the congested, noisy arrival area where I stopped and scanned the crowd until my eyes met my mother's husband. He was already observing me from a distance, which made me assume that he wanted to make sure that I wasn't accompanied by anyone. I looked him in the eyes to make sure that he saw me, and it caused him to quickly look away and pretend not to notice me. In an attempt to indicate to him that I was alone, I moved away from the crowd, then watched as he approached with a grin on his face. In the most friendly voice that I had ever heard, he said, "You look a lot like your mother." I replied, "Depends because some people say I look like my father." "Then I guess it really depends," he replied. There was then complete silence as we made our way toward his vehicle. The first thing that caught my attention was the missing front number plate, which startled me, and I asked "No number plate?" and he responded, "Vehicles here don't carry front number plates." To make sure that he wasn't deceiving me based on his previous lies regarding my mother, I scanned every vehicle inside the parking lot until I was satisfied that he was truthful.

There still wasn't much talking as we drove off, but whenever he spoke, I'd notice that he'd look me in the eyes and speak in a deep tone. I already knew that it was a form of psychological pattern used by many to assert full authority over a person. It starts simple but is very effective with the victim being unaware and within a flash, the person would be easily controlled. Since it was the early stages of meeting me, it was the best time for him to attempt his manipulation.

My eyes were everywhere, familiarizing myself with the area as we drove by a lake almost the size of a channel where a fleet of about five cargo ships was anchored, then drove through a neighborhood that reminded me of a rural area on a Caribbean island. There were wooden homes surrounded by lush green grass , clothes hung from wires and tiny outdoor buildings that left me to wonder if they were all latrines.

Finally, we exited the highway and moved into a residential area enclosed by bricks and wooden homes of excellent quality. Most were concealed by sequoias towered over them. Suddenly, we pulled into a driveway of a yard just inches away from bumping into a sequoia that I did my best to identify, but couldn't. "We're here," he said, and my heart jumped. My eyes scanned the surroundings as the vehicle came to a stop, then without saying a word, I exited and left him behind. The first thing my eyes met was the house number imprinted on a small piece of board just above the entrance of the doorway. "This is it! This is the last place where all my mail was returned from, unopened and stamped "Returned to sender". I said to myself. Completely puzzled as to why he took me to a place where my mother no longer lived, I looked beside me, expecting to see him, but he wasn't. I looked back and saw that he was still seated in the driver's seat of the vehicle, staring ahead in a daze as if bothered by something. I found it to be strange. To me, if someone brings you to their house, you'd expect them to accompany you in instead of them remaining inside their vehicle. As much as I wanted to signal him out, I continued toward the entrance of the doorway where my four-year-old sister quietly stood, awaiting my arrival. Her bold eyes glued onto me as I approached. I smiled at her, but she shyly looked toward the ground. "Hello," I said with the smile still on my face before I squatted to the level of her eyes, but she still didn't answer. Her eyes were still glued to the ground when I asked, "Do you know who I am?" She replied "Yes" in a sweet, Southern accent as she nodded. I gave her a hug, then asked, "Who's inside?" but this time, instead of a response, she looked at me and didn't say a word as if she had taken an oath of secrecy. I panicked, took a deep breath, leaped back onto my feet, and was expected to see my mother's husband still seated inside the driver's seat, but he had already made a secret exit. I was then on my own in a place thousands of miles away from my relatives, but after realizing how far I'd come reminded me that I needed closure at any cost. With my eyes closed, I took one final breath and felt my heart pound against my chest, knowing that the only thing separated me from the woman I hadn't seen in almost 14 years was the door with a curtain hung behind it. With one foot placed inside of the doorway, I stepped forward and my knee quivered, and produced a sensation of numbness that caused me to lose my footing. I immediately stumbled, but I managed to grab a hold of the door knob to prevent myself from falling. "Be careful," my sister said, and I comforted her with a smirk before I hesitantly pulled the curtain to one side, then peeked my head in like a scared 10-year-old child. Expected to see my mother standing there with a smiling face, I was instead met by a dark living room, lacking sunlight by undrawn curtains. Cushions were tossed about on the chairs and on the floor, and a disorganized center table rested on a carpet that badly needed to be vacuumed. There wasn't even the sound of a television, radio, or the chime of a clock. The only thing present was an eerie silence of uncertainty that stopped me completely in my tracks. "This can't be my mother's house. Something has to be definitely wrong here because my mother is a clean and tidy person," I said to myself. I made a 360-degree turn around the room as if I was surveying it, and was trying to make sense of everything. There wasn't anything that indicated her presence. Out of nowhere, an unexpected, low but irritated banging of cookware that sounded like something from the old Hitchcock movie "Psycho" grabbed my attention. I looked at my sister for an explanation, but her eyes were already glued to me with pity as she quietly asked, "Are you scared?" Her question made me believe that she was in a mood to talk, and I nervously responded with a smirk, then asked, "Who's behind there?" For the second time, she didn't respond. I was really beginning to convince myself that she had actually vowed to remain mute on any questions concerning my mother.

My heart thudded steadily against my chest so hard it sent me into a panic mode that caused me to press the palm of my hand over my shirt to prevent it from piercing through my jacket as I ambled across the floor. Finally I got to the archway, stopped, then tilted my head forward. For the second time, I expected to see her awaiting me with a smiling face but instead, I instantly froze like a mannequin with my eyes widened in shock, and utterly dumbfounded. I couldn't even blink. The woman I hadn't seen in almost 14 years appeared unrecognizable and decades older, frailed, and weighed approximately 50 pounds. She appeared as if she was on the brink of death. Confined to a wheelchair that was positioned in front of a sink packed with dirty dishes. The pots were in each of her hands, constantly banging due to the constant trembling of her torso like a woman with Parkinson's. My knees gave out and hit the ground like a falling skyscraper, and produced a loud thud that instantly left me paralyzed with shock. My only sign of life came from my loud, uncontrollable breathing that sounded like an asthmatic patient who was gasping for air inside an emergency room. My mother screamed my name out and then, with her motherly instinct, stretched her arms toward me, and caused the wheelchair to tilt to one side. The wheelchair tipped over, and my four-year-old sister managed to grab it and broke the fall as it softly hit the floor. I helplessly watched my mother drag herself toward me with a stiff, completely motionless waist, and trembling torso that immediately caused tears to stream continuously down my cheeks. With her trembling hands, she pulled me to a sitting position and hugged me. I felt her torso tremble against mine, then she burst out a deafening, uncontrollable scream that almost left my ear permanently impaired.

After a moment of constantly sobbing, I regained my strength and in a cracked voice asked, "What happened?!" She replied, "It's ok, it's ok." "No, it isn't. Everybody needs answers," I said, and she responded, "Don't start any trouble." When she made that statement, I leaped to my feet in anger, and attempted to grab a knife to stab the barbaric animalistic husband, but her trembling hands were powerful enough to restrain me. "Stop it! What is wrong with you? Do you want to get shot? There is no one else here with you. How are you going to get yourself out of here when you don't know the area and you don't have an escape route?" she screamed. I couldn't answer, but as much as I realized her cautioning me made sense, I immediately noticed the psychology behind her husband constantly relocating her into remote areas where she didn't know anyone. It showed me how difficult it must have been for her to escape him.

I thought of contacting the FBI, but needed to remain calm first for a moment to make sure that she was safe. Suddenly, I felt a tap on my shoulder and turned and saw my sister standing over me with a box of tissue. I reached for as many as I could then wiped my eyes, but the tears continued to stream down my cheeks. As I lifted my mother to place her back inside her wheelchair, her weight felt no heavier than a 10-year-old child. She was light as a feather. As I Looked at her. I began to plan her husband's death. I wanted him completely off this planet where absolutely no trace of him could have ever been found.

A short moment after, the bastard entered and my mother begged me to remain calm. Watching her dry the tears from her eyes, proved to me that she was very much under his control, living in complete fear, and had to face this animal daily. He looked at me then said, "I'm taking you to meet my parents," without even asking if I wanted to. I looked at him with my eyes widened in complete shock and with anger stirred inside me. I wanted to jump inside his chest but since my mother had already spoken to me about him having a gun, I wasn't sure if it was concealed on him.

I knew that him offering to take me to meet his parents was nothing more than a psychological attempt to show me that I wasn't the only one who had a sick parent. It was just another way of him trying to have me break the concentration off my mother, but I never responded to him. Instead, I stared at him, then felt my mother's trembling hand inside the palm of my hand, "Go ahead, take the ride," she said. With my eyes fixed on him, I wanted to jump inside of his chest, but somehow managed to constrained myself. After a moment of persuasion by my mother, I gave in only because I knew that she'd be the one to face the consequences.

I exited the kitchen, stepped inside the living room, and made my way toward the front entrance where I stopped behind the curtain and saw him leant before her as she nodded from time to time. From what I observed, it was nothing more than him cautioning her to perform an act in my presence.

On my way toward the vehicle, I stopped with my arms folded in disbelief with my head shaking while staring at the ground in despair. I had the mind of a killer in a state where the death penalty was allowed, and getting away with such an act was next to impossible. I figured that there would be too much evidence against me, and my motive for committing such a crime was quite obvious.

Finally, he exited the house, stopped inside the doorway, then appeared to be having a conversation with my sister. After stepping in the front passenger's seat of the vehicle with my arms folded and head faced forward, he entered but I didn't even acknowledge his presence. "You don't look too good," he said. I paused for a moment then without looking at him said, "My mother was strong and healthy when she left," but he never said a word. As he started the ignition, I asked "What happened?" and for the second time, he didn't respond. I sighed, shook my head, then in a quiet tone said, "It was your responsibility to let us know what was going on," and what I said struck his nerve. His mood instantly changed and he began to babble constantly, but the only words I understood were, "Man, you don't even know what's going on." I put myself inside my mother's shoes and saw how fearful she was of him, but I wasn't and dared him to test me.

At first, he had me questioning myself. My experience with him on the phone gave me no assurance, but I didn't know much about narcissists who many, including me, thought were loud, aggressive, and perceived to be evil. I came to realize that narcissists are also quiet, sneaky, and can secretly deceive you. As a matter of fact, his covert ways could actually fool you into thinking that he was a genuine and generous person. This was the same sneaky, malignant, narcissistic animal who swept my mother off her feet. The same animal who appeared at her workplace almost every day, who she ignored at first, and for some reason gave in due to peer pressure. Unfortunately, she was one of those women who believed in "until death do us part, " which is a dangerous belief that has indeed led many people to their deaths.

As the vehicle pulled out of the yard, there was nothing but silence except for the humming of the engine. My eyes were staring blankly through the window for the entire journey as I thought of how this narcissist had everyone fooled. The fact that all of the mail returned from my mother's present address and was stamped "Return to sender" gave us all the impression that she had moved again and was missing, when in fact, she was living at the present address for all those years. Had we known this, the house would have already been swarmed and invaded and there wouldn't have been any reason for me to go to New York City.

After we pulled up to an area with a few wooden homes about 50 feet apart, without saying a word, I exited the vehicle and followed him inside one of the houses where I was greeted by his mother, a small woman, probably in her 80s, who appeared quite genuine. But trusting anyone inside of that house after seeing my mother's condition wasn't a chance that I was willing to take. "Hello," she said with a smile on her face, then extended her hand for a handshake. At first, I was about to refuse the handshake just to see how they'd react but at the last second, I extended my hand and accepted it. "So, I finally get to meet one of you after all these years," she continued with a smile that was nothing but a fake. I looked at her in awkward silence and wanted to burst out "How much more fake can you be?" If any of them wanted to meet my sister and me, they could have easily done so years ago. First of all, they took regular trips to the Caribbean Island where they were born, which is only a few minutes away from St. Vincent and the Grenadines by plane. They were very much aware of all of my relatives' addresses so for her to make such a statement told me how fake she was. She continued babbling, not realizing that I was listening attentively to every word and after she said that she hadn't seen my mother in ages, my blood ran cold. The distance from where she was living to where my mother was living wasn't too far away. My eyebrows rose, and I asked, "How often do you speak to her over the phone?" Without any form of hesitation she replied. "Everyone gets busy now and then," but I didn't waste my time responding to her poor excuse. "Non sense", I thought to myself.

I was then introduced to her husband who also seemed to be in his 80s or 90s but appeared spaced out, and reclined in a chair just a few feet away. After close observation, I noticed that he lacked mobility. I politely said "Hello" and he replied "Hello." "How are you?" I asked, "Well as you can see, I'm here." I responded with a bob from my head. Everyone's eyes were stuck on me as I was talking to him. They'd expected me to show some form of sympathy due to his lack of mobility, but even though I probably was supposed to, I couldn't because I was still under mental distress after discovering my mother's condition, and up to that point since I'd arrived, not one person took the time to ask how I was doing.

"That's his favorite chair," my mother's husband said, and again, I replied "Hmm," which was the same response he gave me when I asked about my mother's illness.

It didn't take long for me to realize that I was dealing with a tight-knit family, as they were all cheerful around each other, yet my mother was confined to a wheelchair and secluded from all of her family thousands of miles away and who had no idea of her whereabouts.

Anger had gotten the best of me, and to restrain myself from bursting out on anyone, I moved toward an open window with both hands tucked inside my pants pockets and silently stared outside to calm myself.

Minutes later, my mother's husband approached me and asked, "Ready?" I nodded "yes", thinking he was ready to take me back to my mother but instead, he took me over to his brother's wife, the woman who I first spoke with over the phone and who was responsible for making the reunion with my mother possible. The atmosphere there was much more genuine, and I almost became emotional after meeting her, but I managed to control my tears. It wasn't even five minutes into the conversation when my mother's husband said he needed to get back to work and wanted me to remain at the house. "Sure," I replied, but in the back of my mind, I was pretty certain that this was his opportunity to return to the house and caution my mother once more. As he left, I asked the lady to help me find a hotel because it was too impossible for me to sleep at my mother's house out of fear that either I was going to kill him or he was going to kill me. I felt certain that someone was going to die that night.

The lady and I drove for miles and miles across highways and byways in search of the closest hotel, which was a 30-minute drive away from my mother's house and would have cost me an arm and a leg in a taxi each trip. Realizing that the hotels were too far away, she took me back to my mother's house after dark and I noticed his vehicle parked inside the yard. Upon entering the house, my mother was quietly seated on the couch with my sister's head resting on her lap. Their full attention was on a basketball game, which was her favorite sport, and the only thing apart from God that kept her going daily. "Goodnight," I said, and she replied, "Goodnight," but her tone sounded to me that something wasn't right. She pointed toward the bedroom as an indication that he was inside, but it didn't matter to me at that point. I flung my hand as if to say "Whatever," not that I meant any disrespect to her but everything about him was already revealed.

"What did he say to you while I was out?", I quietly asked, as I sat beside her. Instead of a response, she demanded that I go to bed. "Not in this house," I replied, and she looked at me in surprise. I continued, "I'm finding a hotel, even if I have to walk to get there." Just then, her husband came out of the bedroom, and the first thing he asked was, "What do you think of my parents?" With my eyes open in shock and my blood instantly gushing to my head, I wanted to burst out on him, but I was afraid that it would have triggered a migraine. Instead, I shook my head, then said, "They're getting down in age." "Yeah, they are," he replied, and at that moment, my mood changed. It took me a moment before I snapped out of it and when I did, I calmly walked into the kitchen to cool myself down, then returned to the living room and said to my mother for a second time, "I need to get to a hotel." Her husband overheard the conversation and replied in his deep, assertive, demanding tone, "I already prepared a room for you." In the calmest possible tone, I replied, "It's best if I go to the hotel." We went back and forth about it for almost five minutes until he realized that he couldn't break me. Out of frustration, he released a sigh then walked away. I turned toward my mother and with my head shaking said, "He's not going to break me. " She looked at me and said, "You're here all by yourself," and I replied "So are you," then her eyes became watery. I squatted down to the level of her eyes and quietly said, "I'm sorry, but I really can't stay here tonight. I'll end up in the electric chair because I'll kill him." "What will it solve?" she asked. "Your freedom," I responded. "And what about yours?" she asked. Without saying another word, I got to my feet, shook my head, and quietly paced the room until her husband re-entered and asked, "Are you ready?" "Yes, I said" but in the back of my head, I was curious as to what had changed his mind so quickly since I had already known him to be a very overly controlling person.

I have come to realize that a person who is overly controlling never allows a person to make their own decision about anything. Their way is the only way, and they're always planning your decision ahead of you without you even knowing. They always approach you off guard about everything. They're always expecting you to submit to all their demands without any objection and if you resist, they expect you to go into details as to why, then they'll react very negatively toward you and place you on a blacklist.

After kissing my sister good night on the cheeks, I kissed my mother on the forehead only to hear her exhale loudly, which to me was a clear sign of dejection, but I knew she understood that my reason for not wanting to stay for the night was to avoid a fight where someone would have definitely been killed.

The hotel was only a short five-minute drive away, and I just couldn't understand why the lady drove me so many miles away instead of us just going to that hotel earlier in the day. Just after arriving at the hotel, I called one of my aunts who lived in another state just outside of New York, and described everything to her. Even though everyone was in total shock at what I described, my description still couldn't convey the injustice. Everyone had to see my mother for themselves to get a proper picture of a small, fragile woman with the body weight of a 10-year-old who looked decades older, almost folded inside a wheelchair with her body shaking constantly. I quickly ended the conversation before I triggered a migraine, turned the lights off, and then sprawled onto the bed, staring at the ceiling in despair, and wasn't even disturbed by the sliver of light that pierced the partially drawn curtain. Trying to understand how a human being could know that another human being is trapped inside a wheelchair and still never reach out to any of their relatives baffled me. The thought was really beyond my comprehension. I wanted instant revenge. Being in a state infested with snakes and alligators made me think of barbaric ways to murder him. My plan was to tie him up, remove his fingernails and toenails, sprinkle them with sugar, then dump him in a rat-infested area and hope that they would slowly chew on him as he screamed in pain to no avail. After that, I wanted to hand him over on a platter to the alligators and watch them rip him apart before they swallowed him in chunks. To me, that would have been justice for a woman who couldn't help herself.

As the tears streamed down my cheeks, I was angry at God and thought that he didn't deserve to be worshiped by me. I wanted to call Him wicked and evil for allowing such things to happen to a kind, loving woman who didn't deserve such treatment. Instead, I found myself pleading to Him for strength with my eyes opened as I cried continuously into the next morning, sprawled on the bed in the same clothing I wore the previous day.

Still in shock and completely out of it, I couldn't even function properly, but I needed to be strong, knowing that I was my mother's only hope. After I brought myself to a seated position on the bed, I exhaled loudly, shook my head, and tried to figure out my next move. Paranoia had the best of me, convincing me that he was planning to move my mother again to an unknown location, and I panicked, then quickly called the number. My sister answered, then after telling her to let our mother know that I'd be over in a few hours, I called my friend back in New York and assured her that I was ok, then I quickly took a shower.

I decided that it was time to inform the authorities, but for some foolish reason, instead of me calling the FBI, who could have done a thorough background check on everything, I called the police. During my conversation with a female police officer who was almost on the brink of tears, she informed me that they would do everything they could to help but first, my mother would need to cooperate. I assured them that she would, then headed over to the nearby cafeteria where I grabbed something to eat, but after I returned to the room with a loss of appetite, I dumped everything inside the trash.

In no time, there was a voice over the radio that came from outside the door followed by a knock. After peering through the peephole, I saw an armed, uniformed police officer standing in front of the door. "Gimme ah minute," I yelled, then quickly slipped my feet inside my shoes before racing out to meet him. Our conversation was brief. He told me what precinct he was from, then reminded me that they could only assist if my mother decided to cooperate. For the second time, I said "Yes. I'm sure she will"

We exited the hotel side by side beneath a billow of scattered clouds, then made our way inside the police cruiser where screeches of static and voices of dispatchers blared from time to time over the radio. Except for that and the humming of the vehicle engine, there was nothing else but silence. Out of nowhere, an indescribable, strange eerie feeling came over me as if something was about to go wrong. "Was my mother's husband at home, and was he about to confront the officer?" I asked myself before I glanced at the officer's waist to make sure that his gun was still fastened inside its holster. Moments later we pulled into the yard, and the first thing I noticed was that my mother's husband's car wasn't anywhere in sight. To me, that still didn't mean that he wasn't at home. Out of nowhere, a 60-something-year-old neighbor who lived about 20 meters away and who I hadn't seen the day before exited her house. She stood outside of her doorway with both hands on her hips in curious observance.

Just before I stepped out of the car, I released a loud sigh that caught the attention of the officer who was now right behind me and asked, "Are you alright?" "I don't even know," I replied, shaking my head. As we got toward the doorway, the memory of entering the house the day before, unaware of what I was about to expect crossed my mind only this time, I didn't lose my footing. As I turned the door open, instead of being greeted by silence as the day before, I was greeted with loud cheers and thunderous applause from a televised basketball game. Across the room, was my mother seated on the couch with my sister's head quietly resting on her shoulder. That was normal, but apart from that, something felt odd. "Good morning," I said. Just as my mother saw the police officer, her eyes widened in shock and my heart jumped. I thought that something terrible was about to happen, and with my eyes widened in surprise, and without hesitation, my mother burst out in a loud uncontrollable scream, "Get him out! Get him out of here, please. I can't talk to him!" and I yelled back at her, "He's here to help you," but her screaming became louder and louder. I was left in complete shock with my eyes and mouth wide open, and couldn't say a word. Her pleas and tears were all obvious signs of manipulation. In an attempt to help her break away from her husband's spell, I squatted before her, stared her in the eyes and in the calmest voice possible said, "Please, for God's sake just tell him," I begged her, "Please." But she continued, "No, everything is fine. There's nothing bad happening," she cried. I continued to press her and said, "Nothing is going to happen to you. He's here to help you. Just talk to him for God's sake, please," but it was as if my pleas fell on deaf ears as her cries for me to get the officer out of the house continued.

I got back onto my feet and shook my head in disbelief, then looked at the police officer who looked back at me and shrugged his shoulders. "I'm sorry. From my experience, something's wrong but there isn't anything that I can do unless she decides to cooperate with us. I'm sorry." He handed me his card, and told me to call him if she changed her mind. "Thank you," I said, and pocketed the card. I watched him make his exit and knew that I was in for a big challenge. Without saying another word to my mother, I coiled myself on the floor in a corner with my head buried in my lap in disbelief. Everyone was silent, except for the cheering of fans at the basketball game that was being televised.

After what seemed like hours of silence and with my head still buried inside of my hands, I finally broke the silence and calmly asked, "Why?" She replied, "Because it could be one of his friends who dressed like a police officer." Her response caused me to take a deep breath, shake my head, look at her, then softly say, "I'm your son who took the journey all the way from St. Vincent to search for you, and now I'm here to rescue you. You don't believe that I would bring a real police officer to help you?" The more I began to think of it, the more I realized how narcissists condition their victims. It is said that those who are abused still find a soft spot in their hearts for their abusers. They'll forgive and defend them at any cost. From what I saw, there's no doubt in my mind that he had her believe that he would send a friend or possible family members over to the house in pretense of them being police officers. To get more information out of her, I asked a second time in a very calm tone, "What makes you think that I would bring you a fake officer?" Instead of a response, she looked toward my sister as the tears streamed continuously down her cheeks, and I asked, "He threatened to take her away from you, didn't he?" She nodded, "Yes."

Knowing that my four-year-old sister meant everything to her and was all she had while isolated in a place surrounded by his entire family brought tears to my eyes. I got to my feet, crossed the floor, sat beside her, and placed her head on my shoulder. The vibration of her torso trembled against mine as she whispered in my ear, "I'm not allowed to call anyone. Not even the hospital." With my eyebrows raised, I burst out "What?!" before calmly lifting her head off my shoulder to look her in the eyes and asked, "So, how do you get medical treatment?" She replied, "I have to call him first, then he comes over to see what the problem is, then decides whether I get to see a doctor or not." Hearing this sent me in total confusion as I tried to make sense of everything. "So what happens if he's unable to answer his phone whenever you call him?" "Then I'll call a family member of his," she replied. At that point, I'd heard enough and wanted her husband dead. I leaped to my feet in anger and told her that I needed to get back to the hotel. "But you just got here," she said. In an angry tone, I responded, "I can't take this anymore, this is too much for me. There is no one here except my sister taking care of you. None of his family members ever come to visit you, and you're telling me that they get to decide whether you see a doctor or not. Are you serious?!" She never responded. I paused for a moment with the palm of both hands resting on my head, then continued in anger. "The only reason why this man is still alive since I got here is because of the death penalty because I know you'll lose me, then probably go mentally insane. On the other hand, it seems as if you're already mentally insane. It's as if you've already lost my sister and me for the last 14 years so you can live with it, but the sad thing is my sister, at four-years-old, will now be taken away from you and handed over to his relatives." There was no response from her, and I continued. "He's an evil, selfish man who has been killing you slowly for years. He doesn't care one bit about you. All he cares about is his ill father and mother, yet here you're protecting him. You know what? I've already done my part, and there isn't anything left for me to do." She still didn't respond. I squatted down before my sister, stared her deep in her eyes, and whispered. "If anything ever happens to our mother from now on, you call 911 instead of calling anyone else, you hear me?" She nodded, then said, "Daddy said not to go inside that room," as she pointed toward the bedroom that was just behind me. My curiosity piqued. "Hmm," I said to myself. For him to make such a statement meant that there had to be something concealed inside of that room.

Suddenly, all of my focus was on the bedroom, determined more than ever to enter. I had to constrain myself by pressing onto my legs with the palm of my hands to prevent myself from moving. After I exhaled, I shook my head, looked at my mother whose eyes were blankly staring ahead, and said, "I need to leave now.", then I kissed her on the cheeks, kissed my sister on the forehead and with that, I left the house.

A plan was now being orchestrated to enter the bedroom without being noticed by anyone, but knew that it was going to be much more difficult than I could have imagined since the bedroom was facing in the same position as the television.

In less than an hour, I was back at the hotel and saw a card attached to the door handle with a note jotted onto it, "Please see the front desk." Thinking that something was wrong with my mother, I panicked and raced over to the front desk only to hear the lady there inform me that I had a number of missed calls from my mother's husband. I tried to figure out why he didn't just call the house to see if I was there since it was the only place I'd be if I wasn't at the hotel, but I guess it was just one of his strange ways of doing things.

I re-entered the room, bursting my brain as I tried to understand why he didn't just send my mother back to us instead of keeping her in this poor condition. Two reasons crossed my mind. The first, I assumed that there must be a large life insurance payout and the second was all because of control. Narcissists have so much obsession for control that instead of releasing a victim, they'd rather keep that victim hostage and watch them suffer because it's what makes the narcissists feel good about themselves.

Soon after, the phone rang. I answered and heard in an angry dominant voice that was powerful enough to shake the weak, "I called you several times." I stood my ground and replied, "Why didn't you just call your house phone?" Being the controlling, arrogant freak that he was, it was like, "How dare you question me?" "I'm on my way," he said in the same angry tone, then hung up. I began to wonder if anyone told him that I had called the cops. To make sure no one did, I called my mother for a head's up. She assured me that no one did, then she began to panic. "Be careful. I don't want anything happening to you," she said, crying out. I calmly replied, "Please relax. There's nothing to worry about. I may be small, but I can handle myself." Soon, I was startled by a loud bang on the door. After peering through the peephole, I saw him pacing the floor, agitated. Just as I opened, he abruptly said, "I need to talk to you." I calmly replied, "Sure," still curious about his attitude. The manner in which he approached me displayed pure dominance. The way he looked at me, his intimidated tone of voice, and his compelled attitude all displayed signs of a man with an obsession for dominance. We made our way over to the parking lot and just as we got there, all hell broke loose. He burst into anger, "Don't you ever again tell my daughter to dial 911," and just as he said that my blood gushed through my body, I decided that I wasn't taking any crap from him and shot back, "Your daughter happens to be my four-year-old sister who is living with my partially paralyzed mother who is in desperate need of medical attention, and neither you nor anyone in your family is medical personnel." He looked at me with his eyes widened as if no one had ever stood up to him before, then right away his demeanor changed as he burst out, "Ain't one damn thing wrong with your mother. As a matter of fact, she's just lazy. There are a lot of things that she can do, but she's just lazy, that's all." Hearing him say that, transformed me into a completely different person. I lost it, but for some strange reason, my migraine never triggered and I could not have cared less if it did. I burst into a rage. "You obscene language piece of crap," a profanity that I'd never used before. He began to speak so fast that I couldn't understand a word he said. I shook my head with my fist folded in preparation to defend myself if needed and wasn't scared of anything, and even though I was only 5'10" and about 120 pounds, I felt as if I was David standing before Goliath. I yelled out, "Hit me the way you hit her. Come on." He shot back, "Is that what she told you?" I panicked, out of fear that my mother was going to be the one to face his wrath. In a quiet tone, I replied, "She doesn't have to tell me anything. The evidence is right in front of my face." Soon after, I felt a migraine coming on. Then in a soft tone, I said, "You're all about mind control, and you know that one of the easiest ways to control a person is when they don't have anyone else to turn to. That's the reason why you kept moving her from state to state, making sure that she was always around your family while hers are thousands of miles away." I paused for a moment and continued to stare him in the eye but he never responded, knowing that I was speaking the truth. "It's all Stockholm Syndrome, isn't it?" I continued with my eyes kept on him. "You knew she had no one in New York when you swept her off her feet." The guilt appeared all over his face before he sighed, glanced away, then looked back at me, then for the first time, in a soft tone, he replied, "You think you know it all, don't you?" I replied, "I'm old enough to know when a person is being psychologically abused." "Man, you're just a kid," he said. And I responded, "One who's much smarter than you can ever imagine." That silenced him completely as we stared each other off. I watched him re-enter the vehicle and drove away. With my head shaking, I found a seat on the floor with my head in the palm of my hand, then completely broke down.

Hours later, I found myself buried under the covers with tears streaming continuously down my cheeks, knowing how much danger my mother was in. It was something that she just couldn't see as a result of her fear. The crazy thought of me returning to the house in search of his gun to shoot him constantly played out inside of my head, but that was impossible. I got to my feet, pulled the curtain, and stared at the mini-mart and gas station across the street as I fought the urge to enter and purchase a flip knife. Then I remembered several detectives on television stated that attackers often cut themselves during a knife attack, and I was afraid that I'd cut myself and leave my blood evidence at the scene. I also knew that detectives have a way of finding things out. The moment my four-year-old sister told them that her brother came to visit, I would have been suspect number one, even without any blood evidence. All they would have needed to do was to check the hotel camera, which would have shown me leaving the hotel that night. Their vicious interrogation would have torn me apart. I was also in one of the states that still carried the death penalty, and to picture myself inside an electric chair was pretty terrifying. Instead, I shook my head in frustration, knowing that I was left hopeless and alone in a place that I was unfamiliar with, abandoned by the same person I risked my life to rescue, all because she failed to cooperate.

The next day I awoke concerned due to the argument with my mother's husband and me the previous day, then called to make sure that she was ok. She wasn't sounding like herself, and I asked, "What happened?" Instead of responding to my question, she asked, "What did you do?" "Stood up for myself and you," I said. "How exactly did you do it?" she cried out, and I responded, "Relax. We had an argument." She called me by my name and screamed out, "Are you crazy? For Christ's sake, he has a gun," and I responded, "Then let him pull the trigger. In that way, the cops will get involved." She went silently, and I said, "I'm on my way over." She replied, pleading. "Oh no, please don't. I don't want anything to happen to you." I sucked my teeth, then rudely hung the phone up.

In no way was I afraid of her husband because one thing I know about narcissists, they are insecure, manipulative cowards who constantly live in distress and feed off your energy. They cannot feel good about themselves and take pleasure in putting people down to make themselves look and feel good. Once their lies are exposed, they become very offensive, but beating them at their own game is something that frustrates them. Not that I wasn't concerned about my safety, but it wasn't enough to prevent me from going back to the house.

After searching the hotel for anything that could be used as a weapon to protect myself against him if needed, the only weapons available were bed sheets, towels, pillowcases, and a pen next to the bed lamp. I pocketed the pen before exiting the hotel in search of a taxi. There was none and Uber was nonexistent at the time. I decided to wait on the bus, but what I thought would be about a five-minute wait turned into more than an hour of waiting.

My best option was to journey by foot. I strolled on sidewalks, and underpasses as traffic zoomed past me in both directions on a two-way street. Silent walking through the streets with thoughts of my mother swirling inside of my head confused me as to why my surroundings suddenly appeared to look different. I came to realize that I had veered off the main road and onto a narrow, emptied street where there wasn't any traffic. The area appeared lonely and creepy. High grass was on each side of the street and houses were very much apart from each other. "What in the world am I doing here?," I asked myself, then stopped and shook my head in disbelief, knowing that I was far away from the main road. I looked at the closest house to me, which was about fifty meters away, surrounded by trees and an old gate that appeared somewhat rusted. I proceeded toward the gate with the intention of knocking on the house door to ask for permission to call my mother so she'd know that I was on my way. Just as I reached for the gate, it squeked and my mind ran across Freddy Krueger of Nightmare on Elm Street. I said to myself "nope," then thought about how often people went missing each day. I raced away from the gate, then made a u-turn back toward the road, shaking my head in frustration. Minutes back into my walking, the distant sound of a vehicle moving toward me grabbed my attention and caused me to turn. Approaching was a four-wheel drive that moved past me, then made a sudden stop just a few feet. I came to an instant standstill, and stared at the vehicle in a moment of quiet suspense. Without warning, the window on the driver's side slowly lowered to the level of a man's eyes hidden behind a pair of sunglasses. My heart pumped faster and faster as I feared the worst. Right away, I patted my pants pocket to make sure that the pen was still concealed inside of it just in case I needed to use it as a weapon of defense. I was expecting him to exit the vehicle at any moment. Instead, he asked, "are you lost?", which I was sure of to him, that was quite obvious. Knowing my thick Caribbean accent was a giveaway, I decided it was best to remain silent. Instead, I responded by shaking my head "no". "Yes, you are buddy. Ah seen you from all the way up there." He said. At that very minute, fear set in and caused my knees to tremble and wondered if I too was about to disappear after coming to a foreign country in search of someone who was missing for years. I responded with a shrug from my shoulders as I slowly walked toward the vehicle since it was in the path of my direction, then as I got closer, he said "Hop in?" I stopped completely as he continued, "You don't have to be afraid man. I'm not going to do anything to you." What he said concerned me because most of the time, those who say that they'll never hurt you, are always the first ones to do so. During my standstill, it was as if a voice said to me "Please do not go inside of that vehicle." At that point, the driver took notice of my hesitance, and continued, "It's ok, buddy. Hop on in.", Even though the way in which he emphasized the word "buddy" made me uncomfortable, I began to think of my mother's condition. I thought of how nothing was going right for me. I didn't care about anything anymore and didn't even care if my body was reported on the 6 p.m. news. Realizing that there wasn't anything left for me to lose, it was as if the fear left my body. I said to myself "Goodbye world. If this is it, then so be it," then hopped inside of the vehicle. I didn't even care whether I was seated beside a kidnapper or a serial killer at worst. He began to question me about my day and wanted to know where I was from to which I answered truthfully, but remained on alert. When he began to ask about my family, which is something serial killers and cult members do, I became a bit hesitant. The fact that giving anyone details about your ill parents could very well put you at a disadvantage, I hesitated for a bit, knowing that he could use the opportunity to pretend that he was lending support for me to gain his confidence, then later on turn it against me. But then again, I didn't care and began to open up about everything. It turned out that he was a gentleman and took me directly to my mother's house.

My sister was already awaiting me at the door when I arrived. I said "Hello," picked her up, kissed her on the cheeks, then carried her inside where the aroma of cooked chicken lingered. I sucked my teeth, put my sister onto her feet, then my eyes went straight toward the bedroom door that I was prohibited from entering but was very much determined to.

I turned to my sister, and asked, "Did your daddy tell you why he doesn't want me to go inside the room?" and she said "No," but I was very much convinced that for him to make such a statement meant that there had to be something inside that room that he didn't want me to see. The more I thought about it, the more I believed that it had a lot to do with evidence of some sort.

I made my way inside the kitchen and saw my mother seated inside her wheelchair in front of the sink, washing dishes for the second time. Just as she saw me, she dropped the dishes and cried out in panic, "Go back, please, go back to the hotel before something happens to you." In a soft, calm tone, I replied "It's ok, Nothing is going to happen to me, I can assure you that. Don't you worry about my safety. I can handle myself," but she continued on. "He's angry at you for what you did, and I don't want anything happening to you. You're here alone," but as much as I tried to explain to her that I was going to be ok, she wasn't convinced.

I put myself in her position and came to the belief that he had threatened her with his gun as a part of his fear tactic, and that sent me in a rage. Knowing that I had absolutely nothing to lose, I barged over to his bedroom door and violently banged on it, pulled and tugged onto the handle, "Are you there? Why don't you come out if you're inside?" I shouted as my mother pleaded for me to stop, but I got no response, then stormed outside in search of his vehicle but it wasn't anywhere in sight.

After I calmed myself down, I returned to the kitchen and wheeled my mother into the living room, took her out of the wheelchair, then placed her onto the couch. In a quiet tone, I asked, "Did he threaten you with his gun?" She looked at me without responding, and I continued, "Doing nothing about everything that he's doing to you is only making him continue, especially since he's a narcissist. These people never stop. In fact, they can't stop because they are sick, and as much as they know that what they're doing is wrong, they're not going to stop unless you do something about it. They will continue to manipulate you at every chance." She still didn't respond. I paused for a moment, shaking my head, then continued, "You have this man inside the palm of your hands, and you can easily break him. He's not as bad and as scary as you think he is. All you need to do is to call the cops. Please, let me call them for once," I said in a soft tone. "No," she said, and I looked at her in silence, shook my head, handed her the television remote, then returned to the kitchen where I opened the oven and saw a baked chicken in a dish. I sucked my teeth, shook my head in silent anger, then beneath my breath, said, "There's just no way that this woman could be serious."

I got back onto my feet in complete silence, paced the kitchen floor with my arms folded, took a deep breath, then returned to the living room and asked, "What's his work number?" She replied, "I can't give it to you." As upset as I was, I calmly said, "Listen, this is all abuse and he's never going to stop unless the law gets involved. A person tests you first to see what they can get away with and he realizes that he's been getting away with what he's been doing to you for all these years. He's never going to stop." She never said a word, then I squatted down before her, softened and continued, "Let me call the police one more time, please, and all you have to do is tell them exactly what is going on. I promise you that you'll be safe, and so will my sister and me. Everyone will be safe." Instead of a response, she looked at my sister who was standing right behind me, then shook her head "No." I calmly re-entered the kitchen, stood over the sink filled with dirty dishes, shook my head emotionally before dropping to my knees and irritated my injured knee, then broke down. Within seconds, my sister appeared with the same box of tissue and touched my shoulder with the palm of her hand. Instead of pulling a tissue, I hugged her as the tears streamed down my cheeks.

After a moment, I broke the hug and sent her back into the living room. I got back onto my feet and felt the pain in my injured knee. "Oh no," I said to myself, knowing that I had to walk for about 30 minutes back to the hotel.

Suddenly, an idea came to mind, and I quickly picked the telephone up and dialed the number on the card given to me by the police officer. Just as I spoke, he recognized my voice. "Hey, how is everything?" he asked. "Nothing changed, but what if my sister speaks on everything that she sees?" I asked. He replied, "Unfortunately, we're still going to need your mother's side of the story." I paused for a moment, thanked him, then ended the call.

I pondered for a moment before removing the baked chicken from the oven, and saw what looked like a dishwasher. Out of curiosity, I asked "Does this thing below the sink work?" "Not really," she answered, and I shook my head, washed the dishes by hand, then rejoined her and my sister inside the living room.

My mind was constantly fixed on the bedroom that I was forbidden to enter but was pretty much determined to find a way in. What time does he come home?" I asked. "In the next hour or less," my mother answered, then asked, "Why?" "Curious," I responded, then found a seat beside her to question her about some things that we all needed answers to. Even though we knew that she hadn't abandoned us, we still wanted to hear it out of her mouth. I took one deep breath, released, looked at her, then asked, "What was your reason for abandoning us?" She looked at me with her eyes widened in shock as if she was offended, called my name then said, "I am your mother. I had you and your sister at a very young age and never abandoned any of you then. What makes you think that I will after all these years?" At that point, there was no response from me and she continued. "Do you really think that I'd ever do something like that to any one of you?" she asked. "You tell me." I replied, then she went on, "Stop it! I'm really surprised that you would say something like that. You and your sister were still in high school when I asked for your documents, and as soon as I got them I handed everything over to him. When I received the mail from immigration and saw that neither you nor your sister's name was anywhere on the paper, I found it very strange because you were both in high school at the time." What she said got my attention. I switched the conversation, got back onto my feet, shaking my head, then asked "Why didn't you just run away from him or something? your sister saw right through him and told you that you needed to run." "So that he could have hunted me down and killed me?" Hearing her say that showed me how much she was conditioned with fear. I shook my head once again, sucked my teeth, then allowed her to continue. "It wasn't until after we left New York that I really saw his true colors, and at the time, I was beginning to get sick so there wasn't anything I could have done. As much as he promised to be there for me, he never was." "911 is always a phone call away. Why not just call them?" I said. She replied, "You don't understand, do you?" "Tell me, because it's hard for me to believe that you never had a window of opportunity to escape." I said. "Eyes were constantly on me, and there were always threats from him," she replied. With the tone of my voice slightly raised, I said, "There are always signs before a lot of things happen, and he must have shown you many. The first sign was when he moved you away from all your friends and family and took you around all of his. He kept changing telephone numbers whenever anyone called you, and you couldn't see it was his way of controlling you? Once a person sees that you do nothing about something the first time, they'll do it a second time before continuing." She never responded and I continued, "He's nothing but an evil, sick, wicked bastard who had it all planned out from the beginning. It was never about you." She became timid. I still needed to keep in consideration that she was my mother and that I needed to treat her with respect, so I toned my voice down before I continued. "He's not going to change. What you see is what you're going to keep getting. Miss Maya Angelou once said, 'When people show you who they are, you have to believe them.' He has been showing you who he is all this time, a lying, manipulative, overly controlling animal in the body of a human who doesn't care one bit about you." She still didn't respond and I continued. "Look around, the only person you have taking care of you is my four-year-old sister who should probably be in school. You don't have a nurse's aide, he doesn't take care of you, and neither does his family who doesn't even visit or call you." I paused for a moment then continued. "Do you know that many in your family thought that you were dead? What if he decides to move again and we never find you next time?" Tears began to stream down her face but instead of stopping, I pressed on, knowing that I had her. My years of obsession with detective television shows taught me that if I needed her to talk to the authorities, then I needed to keep pressing. I decided to use a different tactic by reaching for the telephone receiver and kept it in the palm of my hand, looked her in the eyes then continued, "All it takes is three digits, 9-1-1, that's all it takes and in no time, cops will be swarming this house. They will listen to every word that you have to say. They'll feel your pain and understand what you're going through, then you'll be completely free, but you have to tell them everything." She didn't respond, so I continued, "No need to be scared of anything. I'm your son. I'm here with you. My reason for coming here is to get you out of this mess." Finally, she asked, "What if no one believes me?" I quickly replied, "They will, and you'll be taken care of. Even if they have to place you in a home for battered women, you wouldn't be there for long because I'll head back to New York, find a job, save as much money as I can, then figure something out from there." Suddenly, the telephone receiver began to beep. It was as if something came over her as she took a deep breath, then asked my four-year-old sister to head into the kitchen to make her a sandwich and get her a glass of juice. At that moment, I felt that I had convinced her to speak, but then she asked me to put the receiver down. With my eyes and mouth open in shock, I belted out "What?!" My sister made her way into the kitchen, then in a soft tone, my mother said, "Just put the receiver down, go into that room, and you'll see some very important documents. Write all the information down, then contact an attorney when you get back to New York." My eyes lit up, after realizing that I now had the opportunity to go into the room that I was forbidden from entering. "What room?" I asked just to make sure. "That room behind you." She replied. I paused for a moment and asked, "What about you talking to the authorities?" "Just do as I say. Please." She responded. I stared at her for a moment before turning the doorknob of the bedroom door as it slowly twisted, then made my way inside the room and stopped. What I thought was a bedroom seemed more like a disorganized room with boxes upon boxes and junk everywhere, but what intrigued me was something that I'll refer to as a filing cabinet that I believed had evidence of something concealed inside. It interested me. I reached for the documents my mother asked me to get, and looked at them, but for some reason replaced them, then stared at the same thing I'll call a filing cabinet with my arms folded before I curiously approached it. After stopping for a moment, I placed both hands on my hips and stared at the top drawer silently, exhaling as loudly as I could. Battling the temptation to pull it open, it didn't take long for anxiety to get the best of me. Then without hesitation, I reached for it and slightly pulled on it, but it turned out to be much more difficult to open than I thought. It didn't even budge. I stopped for a moment, took another deep breath, reached for it a second time, then violently wrestled it, tugged it from side to side as piles of aged and crumbled paper rustled against the side of the draw. Suddenly, it squealed, and slightly opened, revealing stacks of dried, aged crispy paper, scattered and improperly filed. I began to meticulously search the letterhead of each document for a while, but found nothing of interest. I was about to give up, but something about his statement not to go inside the room just didn't sit well with me. For the second time with my arms folded, I paced the floor, then decided to continue. All I saw were old receipts and bills from prior years that I thought should have been tossed but since they weren't, I was convinced that old documents concerning my mother had to be among them. I continued my search and the first documents of interest that caught my attention were sent from my aunt back in St. Vincent with my mother's signature scribbled onto the signature line. To me, this was now useless but piqued my interest enough to continue. What I saw next froze me in my tracks with my mouth and eyes widened, I said "Oh my God," then with my trembling hands, nervously reached for a stack of unsealed and unstamped mail addressed to my sister and me years prior with the same awkward handwriting. In that mail was every telephone number and new addresses scribbled with the same awkward handwriting that informed us each time my mother moved, but not once did any of them mention anything about her illness. The notes that grabbed my attention were written in my Christmas and birthday cards with cash tucked away inside them with the message, "To my dearest beloved son, happy birthday, and merry Christmas to you, I love you very much, be patient, everything will work out, and I will see you and your sister very soon." All the evidence was now in front of my face. It was all the proof needed to show that my mother had never and would have never abandoned either my sister or me. I was pretty sure that she never had thought those mail was just a few feet from where she sat each day.

I went into detective mode once more and began to compare all her handwriting, signatures, and photographs. As I put everything together, I realized a possible timeline of when she became ill. The more I thought about it, the more I saw an isolated woman who was silently pleading in pain for an escape from an evil, sick, overly controlling, psychotic animal, but was too afraid of leaving him.

I shook my head, completely dismayed before I found a seat on the floor. Completely spaced-out, I stared at the sliver of light from the sligh cracked open door ahead, and had lost track of time until my mother screamed my name. Pleading for me to exit the room, she screamed, "He's home, come out now. What's taking so long!" she cried out. I was at a point where confronting him or physically battling him wasn't something I was afraid of. My only concern was him retaliating against her and for that reason, I once again began to wonder how in the world could I murder him without going to prison. Everything was against me, and escaping any murder charges was very much impossible.

Unexpectedly, the door squeaked, and as the sliver of light expanded inside the doorway, the small figure of my sister appeared as my mother's screaming continued, pleading with me to get out. "Daddy's home," my sister said, and without saying a word, I placed my index finger over my lips in a silent gesture, then watched her exit the room. I was fed up and angry and wanted him to catch me inside of the room so that there would have been a confrontation about the letters he never posted that made many in my family believe that my mother was dead.

Finally, I shook my head, and without writing any of the information my mother told me to write, I replaced everything inside the drawer, then calmly re-entered the living room where my mother was seated in panic. "What took you so long?" she asked as I pulled the window curtain and saw her husband unloading groceries from inside the vehicle. "Nothing," I said, then made my way toward her. He entered the house at the same time and asked, "How are you doing?" As much as I wanted to remain mute, I answered, "Good," out of fear for my mother. Deep inside, I wanted to confront him about everything. As he made his way inside the kitchen, my mother asked, "Did you get everything?" I shook my head "No," but replied, "I saw all the letters that were never mailed to us, along with all the documents where the names of my sister and me were removed." She looked at me in shock with her eyebrows raised, then comforted me by placing her trembling hands inside the palm of my hands, and said, "It's ok. Just get an attorney when you get back to New York."

It took me a moment to get myself together mentally and just to get everything off my mind as I was still angered by the mail. I said to my mother, "It's getting dark, and I have to go now." She looked at me, then asked, "You mean you're not even going to spend one night here?" I replied, "Because of what I just saw, I would kill him quicker, so just tell him for me that I'm gone." I kissed her and my sister each on their cheeks, then with a sweater hung over my neck, exited the house and entered into the verge of darkness, shivered by an unexpected, lingered chill that quickly penetrated my body, and caused goosebumps to appear in the blink of an eye. I slipped the sweater over me, slid my ungloved hands inside the pockets of my pants. The chill wasn't something I was expecting at all, since I was in a southern state, close to the tropic of Cancer. My almost clean, shaved head was exposed, but to think of the bus schedule drove me crazy, and I wasn't going to take the same chance I took a few hours earlier waiting on a bus that took over an hour to arrive. Neither was I going to return to the house. With both hands tucked inside of my pocket, I continued on.

I continued on, utilizing every vehicle that passed me in each direction as my guide to prevent myself from going off track for a second time. Halfway into my journey, I felt an unbearable pain inside my injured knee that brought me to a halt and almost to the brink of tears. "Aye," I said, flinching before massaging my knee with the tips of my chilly fingers. I sighed, shaking my head in agony. My eyes glanced at every passing vehicle in hope that out of mercy someone would stop and offer a ride, but I was simply ignored. Suddenly my toes felt numb and the soles of my feet felt heavier than normal. There was a tingling sensation along with pain at the tip of my toes, and the blood inside my head felt as if it was about to turn into an icicle. Without any experience in the medical field, all it took was my common sense to realize that it was possible in the early stages of frostbite, and I knew that I needed to keep moving.

With my eyes kept on the hotel's logo towered above its structure through fog from a mile away, I released a loud sigh. The air left my mouth and instantly transformed into a twirl of fog before it scattered into the gloomy atmosphere, then I limped my way toward the hotel as fast as I could. My heart pounded faster and faster as plumes of fog continuously exited my nostrils with every breath. The unbearable, excruciating pain shot through my injured knee like a tremor and caused me to hop for the rest of my journey. Within an hour or more, I made it back to the hotel.

With stiff, frozen fingers fumbling inside my pocket, I retrieved the key card, then awkwardly swiped it across the key card reader, entered the room, then turned the shower on to as warm as I knew my body was able to withstand, then raced into the shower and felt the warmth of the water hit my body as I slowly defrosted. Later on, I came to find out that it was one of the dumbest things that I had ever done.

Later that night, a pound on the door caused me to jump. As I looked through the peephole, I saw my mother's husband calmly standing there with both hands inside his pocket. I wasn't sure if his presence meant there would be a confrontation about me entering the room. After thinking about it for a moment, I wasn't in the mood for an argument or any conversation. What I saw hours earlier made me pass my boiling point, and all I wanted was to be alone. After not answering him, I watched from behind the slightly drawn curtain as he made his way back over toward his vehicle, then reclined on the driver's seat for a moment before he took off. About 10 minutes later, the phone rang. From the corner of my eye, the light pulsed continuously, but I was already under the covers staring at the ceiling in a vacant gaze and just couldn't be bothered.

That night, I laid in bed in complete darkness. My eyes were widely open as thoughts of my mother ran through my head. To think that even while living in New York City she never tried to escape when all of the madness started and she was warned by two of her sisters to run but never did, beats me, and still does to this day. My hate and anger toward her husband were like mantras. Everything had gotten to me so much that I began to think that my entire mission was nothing but a failure and a complete waste of time. The years of sleepless nights back in St. Vincent and the Grenadines when many thought that she was dead to the excruciating pain and the consecutive days of mental pain I endured all started to get to me. To know that my four year-old-sister was the only one taking care of her brought tears to my eyes. Knowing that not for once did my sister ever complain, hesitate, or refuse to assist our mother in any way touched my heart.

Just two days into my visit, I was alone in a country where those who vowed to serve and protect couldn't do anything unless my mother decided to cooperate. Her refusal to do so made me believe that she was enjoying her years of abuse. Throwing in the towel was my other option, but then I remembered how well a narcissist chooses their victims. Never for once should any person believe that they chose a narcissist. It's the narcissist who chooses you. They'll test you in search of a weak point and wherever they see vulnerability, that's exactly where they'll attack. They're egocentric, sadistic, and have no remorse for hurting others as they lack empathy. They think that the world owes them and are convinced that they're superior toward others. My mother was very empathetic toward everyone, and I'm sure it was something that he noticed from the very beginning, plus she had no relatives around her.

For the next two days, I locked myself inside the hotel to rest my swollen knee and isolated myself from the world.

Apart from the phone calls made to my mother twice each day, I had absolutely no contact with anyone except for going to the cafeteria at the gas station across the street where all of the beverages were much cheaper than at the hotel. Numerous phone calls went unanswered unintentionally due to the phone accidentally being on silent, but I managed to answer one call that was indicated by the pulsing green light on the receiver. "Hello," I said, then the caller said, "Morning." For a moment, I was confused because the caller had a thick Southern accent. "Morning," I replied, curious as to who the caller was. "How are you," the caller continued. "I'm fine," I replied, which was nothing more than a lie. Still puzzled, I listened and the caller continued. "I want to invite you to church this coming Sunday. I'd like to introduce you to my husband." I was still confused until I realized that it was the same lady who made the reunion with my mother possible. At first, I hesitated due to the pain in my knee, but I figured that Sunday was two days away and I wanted to meet her husband. He was the brother of my mother's husband, who I was sure was the complete opposite. "Sure," I replied. "Ok, I'll pick you up," she said. "Sounds good," I replied, then ended the call.

The church was a completely different experience. The atmosphere was very much high-spirited. Many were cheering, laughing, and mingling with each other as family. In no time, I was introduced to the woman's husband who seemed much friendlier than my mother's husband. Everything from his charm to the way in which he spoke appeared to be different and genuine. I quietly found a seat alone on an empty bench and looked around the room, curious as to how many of them knew my mother. While looking, I noticed that the lady who brought me seemed to be very close to a girl who was no more than 15 years old. I thought, "If she happens to be a friend of my sister, then maybe, there is a possibility that I may be able to get some information out of her." I said to myself. In my head, a plan was immediately put together to single her out.

After moments of quietly sitting with my eyes closed, almost to the brink of daydreaming, a familiar voice said, "Let's pray." I opened my eyes, sat up, and saw my mother's brother-in-law standing in front of the pulpit. As everyone closed their eyes, mine remained open, not wanting to miss anything. After a long prayer where many spoke in tongues, raised their hands, and shouted the name of God, he asked that everyone turn to a particular chapter in the Bible. That's when my heart dropped. I crouched back into my seat and stared at the floor in despair, shaking my head. I came back to a sitting position, bobbed my head with my arms folded, then buried my face inside the palm of my hand. It was as if a dagger had just pierced me through the chest. My few minutes of smiles and laughter had once again turned into distress and at that moment, I trusted no one except for the lady. There I was isolated in a place I knew nothing about or anyone for that matter, being forced to listen to the gospel preached by the brother of the man who physically and mentally abused my mother. Leaving was not an option. I was miles away, didn't have enough money in my pocket for a taxi, and was without a cellphone. Realizing that everything I thought about that family being tight-knit, and only cared about themselves was confirmed. Without uttering a word, my mind went completely blank for the entire service until a lady tapped me on the shoulder and said, "Pastor asked that everyone step forward." That's when I snapped out of it. Adults and children as young as five years old moved toward the pulpit as I got to my feet without saying a word or engaged in any form of eye contact and quietly joined the line. He stepped down from the pulpit and began to pray as many with their eyes closed lifted their hands and shouted the name of the Lord. My eyes were kept open, quietly observing everything about him. Everyone was asked to step forward, and they followed his command in a synchronous motion as if in a trance. A single tap from the tip of his fingers onto their foreheads sent them into a tremble of original dance moves yet to be copied, as if overtaken by a seizure, then they fainted backward into the open hands of two awaiting men who broke their falls to prevent them from hitting the floor. It was something I'd seen on television numerous times. A relative back in St. Vincent and the Grenadines had cautioned me never to fall when a preacher taps me on the forehead. According to him, everyone who falls to the ground only does so because they see everyone else is doing it.

Finally, it was my turn and as much as I wanted to step out of the line and walk back toward my seat, I thought of how awkward it would be and how everyone would have looked at me differently. On the other hand, they were all people I wasn't going to ever see again for the rest of my life, so not that it meant much to me. Finally, I stepped toward him, stared him in the eye for a few seconds and was very much tempted to ask, "How could you stand there, and allow my mother to suffer like that by your brother? And you consider yourself to be a man of God?" Instead, my eyes were kept on him. He began to pray, then tapped my forehead with the tip of his finger. I felt the hands of the two men behind me rested on my back in preparation to break my fall, but I didn't budge. Instead, I stood firm and stared him in the eyes, and he slightly looked away. Believing that his second tap was going to be more powerful than the previous, I stood as if I was sturdy, in preparation. He raised his hand for a second time, and that time his entire wrist was wide open, which made me suspicious that he was about to tap my forehead much harder. With my body tense, in preparation for an impact, the palm of his hand hit my forehead with a more powerful tap than before. I jolted back and forth like a springboard without saying a word. I broke the stare, then found my way back to my seat. A burden of uneasiness weighed me down as I humbly sat in silence, staring toward the floor. A sense of stare toward me caused me to quickly glance across and saw the same girl who I thought was about 15 years old staring at me, but pretended not to see her. I had very high expectations of questioning her after the service, but unfortunately, there wasn't anything I got from her except for an introduction.

About half an hour later, I got to my mother's house and was hit with the aroma of food. "How was church?" she asked. "Good, but I had no idea what the service was about since my thoughts were elsewhere after realizing that your brother-in-law was the pastor," I said, then shook my head. I was about to go deeper into the conversation and ask if he'd ever involved the authorities about what was taking place but instead sighed, then continued. "My mind was far away, but the congregation may probably hate me by now." I said. "Why?" she asked, looking at me in shock. "Well, I was tapped on the forehead twice, but I refused to fall back, and that wasn't something that anyone expected," I replied. She burst out laughing, and even, to me it was odd, seeing her laugh for the first time since I got there, made me feel good. We began to reminisce about so many things, and it was unbelievable to see how much she remembered. "You still only eat crackers and rice?" she asked, I looked at her stunned, then laughed, and she continued, "You only enjoy eating bread when it's hot or warm, and if the outside of the bread isn't white enough, you never eat it. You like your rice and macaroni prepared not too soft and if they stick together, you will leave it right there. You picked out every piece of onion and garlic from out of everything before you started eating, and you would only eat Jackfish and Robin when they were fried," she said. I replied, "That's because they are too coarse." She continued. "You also hated tea and coffee and only drank juice, sorrel, coconut water, and mauby. I couldn't even get you to eat vegetables or even provisions. You were not a fan of peanuts and when it came to breadfruit, you only ate it roasted and fried. I had no idea what you had against Quaker oats and cornmeal because no matter how hungry you were, you never ate them. I always used to tell others not to force you into eating anything that you never wanted to eat." I laughed and shook my head, then made my way inside the kitchen where I was startled. Just like that, my few minutes of laughter suddenly turned to sadness after I saw all four burners on the stove occupied by a pot. One after the other, I lifted each cover of the pots and looked inside. There were rice and peas, an assortment of vegetables, stewed fish, stewed beef, then after opening the oven I saw macaroni pie and meatloaf. I shook my head in distress before finding a seat on the floor with my face buried in the palm of my hands. "This is complete madness," I said to myself. How in the world a woman can be doing all this from a wheelchair is beyond me. I got back to my feet, calmly returned to the living room, and asked, "Did someone cook all this for you?" "No, why?" she asked. "You're not supposed to be doing this," I said. "How else am I supposed to eat?" she asked. "It is his job to find someone to do these things for you," I said. "But he isn't doing it, so what am I supposed to do?" I burst out, "Tell the authorities like I keep saying to you. This is madness," then there was complete silence except for the commentator's voice on the television set.

Angry and frustrated, I made my way over to the couch, and reclined with my eyes closed. After a moment I said, "Let me call the cops one more time, please," but she never responded. I lifted my head, and came to a sitting position, then continued, "I will ask them to send a female police officer this time who will understand you more than I'm sure most men will." She stared at me for a moment, then quietly responded, "I just don't know who to trust." "Me. your son, who came here to rescue you. All you need to do is talk." I said. "And I may never see your sister again because the authorities will hand her over to his family," she said. Without me uttering another word, everything went silent once more except for the television.

Moments later, a jingling sound of keys from the living room entrance caused me to recline back onto the couch with the palm of my hands resting behind my head, and my eyes looking straight ahead without blinking. Her husband entered, and it was as if a cloud of darkness appeared from nowhere and haunted the entire room. I felt sick, shook my head with my eyes closed, and did my best to avoid him, but then he asked, "How are you?" "Not too good," I replied. "Problem?" he asked. The urge to confront him about everything crossed my mind but saw my mother's eyes widen as she shook her head in a motion that signaled me to remain quiet. After a short pause, I calmly responded, "Life, I suppose," and that was the end of the conversation.

He headed straight for the kitchen, and I looked at my mother. "He didn't even ask how you were doing," I said. "You shouldn't make everything bother you," she replied, and I continued, "But it's as if you're not even here, and he's mad at you for being in the position you're in. Since I've been here, I've never seen him ask how you're doing or if you needed help in any way." As much as I wanted to get up and leave, I sighed, shook my head, then reclined back onto the couch with my arms folded in silence.

Soon after, he returned and sat at the dining table with a large plate of food, and up to that point, he still hadn't even asked my mother how she was doing or if she needed any kind of assistance to adjust her sitting position or anything. All of her help came from my four-year-old sister, which was something I'd noticed from the first day I got there. To me, this was all child abuse since my sister should have been living the life of a child instead of doing house chores. Without hesitation, I asked, "You're not going to ask my mom if she's ok or if she needs any adjustment in the chair or something?" My mother widened her eyes in shock and motioned me continuously to stop, but I continued. "I mean, you're dealing with a woman who can't help herself." Without even turning to look at me, he replied, "She's ok." I wanted to say a lot more about what was taking place since I got there but again, I was worried about the consequences that my mother would have faced after I was gone. She was so psychologically damaged that he convinced her that he was her only hope, which is something a narcissist does after isolating you from your family. I stared at him silently as he began to eat, and it was the most disgusting chomps and slurps I've ever heard from anyone. I had enough and kissed my mom and sister on the cheeks, then told him that I was leaving.

Back at the hotel, I took a quick shower before tucking myself beneath the blanket in the still of darkness, dazed at the off-light embedded at the bottom of the television set as if it was the only visible object inside the room. Except for the faint, murmuring sounds that came from the radio positioned at the head of the bed, everything else was nonexistent. I shook my head from time to time, knowing the seven days that I had spent in that state tortured me. Accepting that the authorities couldn't help unless my mother was willing to talk bothered me constantly. Even though after realizing how damaging psychology could be, the experience left me at a point where all I wanted, was to be in a world Isolated, undisturbed, where I would be able to concentrate on the positive sides of life, but that was very much impossible because each time I closed my eyes, images of my mother seated inside her wheelchair and her trembling torso crawling toward me, played inside my head. I opened my eyes, placed the pillows over my face, and rolled from side to side in despair before breaking down in tears. At that moment, I wished that I had access to a computer capable enough to erase every bit of memory on everything that I saw, as the tears streamed down my cheeks.

The tension was so uncontrollable that it forced me to exit the hotel room in search of a view from the surroundings, in hope that it would ease my mind, but the emptied streets and distant lit homes in a suburb probably the population of a New York City office reminded me too much of a horror movie. I had no choice but to return to the room and sat on the floor in an unfocused stare at the television, into the following morning as the faint rising of sunlight met me still seated on the floor.

After putting myself together, I limped the half-hour journey to my mother's house. Just as I got there, the first thing that came out of her mouth was, "Go and fix yourself something to eat." "Huh," I said, looking at her for a minute before I asked, "How do you know that I didn't eat?" She replied, "Because you look as if you've been up all night, and I know that you didn't eat breakfast at the hotel because you don't eat muffins and things that I know they have there." "Hmm," I replied, still wondering how she knew that I was up all night. I made my way inside the kitchen and saw the sink loaded with dirty dishes. That brought me to an instant freeze with my eyes and mouth opened in shock, then I yelled, "Are these dishes from last night?" "Some are," she yelled back, and I shook my head. Without saying another word, I cleaned them all, tidied the kitchen, then returned to the living room and reclined inside of the chair across from where she was seated with my eyes closed. I wanted to tell her again and again how much of a control freak her husband was, but doing so was very much impossible for a woman who didn't even realize that she was suffering from Stockholm Syndrome.

"Does he take lunch to work?" I asked, still reclined in the chair with my eyes closed. "Not really, why?" she asked. "Thinking out loud," I replied, then shook my head in silence. "Boy, if I had absolutely nothing to lose, I'd poison him," I said. She took her eyes away from the television set and looked at me in shock with her eyes widened, then I continued, "But I looked at enough detective shows to know that everything will be pointed at me, and I'll be caught. Every container inside this house will be tested for traces of poison and because of your lack of mobility, my sister's age, my motives, the 911 calls, and the confrontation at the hotel will all be enough to convince the authorities that I was the guilty one. I mean, this is just complete madness." The word "confrontation" caught her attention, and she asked, "What confrontation did you have with him?" I replied, "Just a young boy defending his mother." She called me by my name, then said, "I warned you already about what could happen to you. You need to stop because you are here alone," and I quickly responded, "The things that I'll allow people to do to me are not the things that I'll ever allow anyone to do to you, my wife, or kids if I had any. To be honest, it's the electric chair that's really preventing me from murdering him." She became silent, and I continued. "Everything about him is psychological and manipulative. Why do you think that he never came inside the house after he picked me up from the airport that day, then whisked me out of the house to meet his parents, huh?" She still didn't respond, and I kept on going. "The psychology was simple. He knew that I would have been shocked after seeing you, but wasn't sure how I'd react since it was the first time he was meeting me. After he figured that I was calm enough, he appeared from nowhere. For me not to feel too badly about your condition, he took me to meet his sick father, all to show me that I am not the only one who has a sick parent." I stopped for a moment as she quietly looked at me, then I continued. "I'm no longer the little 10-year-old you left back home. I know when people are using psychology, but I always keep my mouth shut and let them do what they want to do because a person's actions tell you everything that you need to know about them. Him telling me that you're lazy even though you're sitting inside a wheelchair tells me exactly what he thinks of you, plus you're inside his domain. It's only a matter of time before he finishes you off completely." Suddenly, an idea came to mind, and I asked, "Can I switch the channel for a bit?" "Sure," she said. I reached for the remote and began to switch from channel after channel in search of any programs that were concerning "missing people, spousal abuse, people held hostage, murder, or any program that pertained to her condition to see if by looking at any would have made her speak to the authorities. There was none. It appeared that her husband was smart enough to make sure that such programs were never televised because all there were, were mainly sports channels, food network, and home improvements.

After getting back to the hotel around 3 p.m., tired and sleepy, knowing that it was my final day, the crazy thought of me returning to the house to pack a few of her and my sister's things, and bringing both of them back to the hotel crossed my mind. I quickly leaped to my feet and was limping my way over to the house, when five-minutes into my journey convinced me that everything was driving me insane. First of all, pushing a woman in a wheelchair near a busy street with a four-year-old beside her was going to get everyone's attention. I would have then been slapped with at least 25 years for kidnapping while her husband would have been walking free to continue abusing her. Her husband was the one who needed to be charged with kidnapping and slavery. From my observation, everything was quite obvious even before she was ill. It was as if she was being programmed 24 hours each day, but it still puzzled me as to how women in those conditions can still find a soft spot in their hearts for their abusers.

After hours of passing out without even realizing, the rhythmic, tapering sound of the rain that was hitting the window awoke me the next morning, which happened to be my final day in that State. Hindering one final visit was on my mind, but the heavy rain delayed me for a much longer period than expected. The wasted time caused me to pace the floor back and forth in frustration, shaking my head as I sucked my teeth from time to time. Just as the rain stopped, I called her. "Is he there?" I asked. "No," she responded. "Then, I'm on my way," I said, and hung the phone up.

Within an hour, I was at my mother's house, looking at her with her eyes flooded with tears and my four-year-old sister comforting her. My heart dropped, thinking that her husband had done something to her. "What happened?" I frantically asked, and she replied "I don't know when I'll be seeing you again." Her answer caused me to breathe a sigh of relief, then after sitting beside her, I said, "Well, consider yourself between St. Vincent and the Grenadines and New York City so, that means I'm only two and a half hours away in each direction." She didn't know that plans were already in preparation for my return visit along with family members who were persistent enough to demand her justice. She placed her head on my shoulder, and I gave her a comforting hug as her torso trembled against me. The years she spent with my sister and me during her healthy days flashed right across my mind and caused me to cry. Her tears drenched the shoulder of my T-shirt and I couldn't help but have as much pity as I could toward her. The urge to press her one final time to call the cops crossed my mind, but getting to the airport within the next few hours was my main goal.

Just then, her husband entered and asked, "How are you getting to the airport?" "I've already arranged for a taxi," I said. He paused for a moment, looked at me, then said, "I was thinking of dropping you." He got no response, and walked away, then my mother gave me the look as if to say, "Please accept the ride." To avoid any problems, knowing that it was my final hours before I saw her again, I accepted the ride. Within a minute, he returned to the living room and said that he needed to take me shopping, which startled me. As much as I wanted to refuse his offer, the look on my mother's face for a second time said otherwise. After a moment of sighs, eye-rolls and head shaking, I accepted the ride. Just as he stepped away, I reminded her that it was all a psychological game. The idea of him taking me shopping was only for him to try his best to leave me with a good impression of him after I got back to New York, but there was just too much to convince me otherwise.

Two hours later, we found ourselves at the mall, inspecting sneaker after sneaker without any form of interest. I was never known to be a materialistic person so his shopping offer had no effect on me. I wasn't going to allow him to think that purchasing me a pair of brand name sneakers meant that I was going to forget about every terrible thing he had done to my mother. We moved from store to store but fortunately, most of the clothing was three times my actual size, which was the way most males wore their clothing at that time. Me dressing like that meant that I would have been walking around looking like an inflated balloon. "They're too big," I said as I inspected T-shirt after T-shirt until I noticed a sign that was hanging from a door that read "T-shirts $1.99." I pointed toward it and knew that they were knock-offs, but didn't care.

All I needed was for him to feel good, so I grabbed a few along with two sweaters, then that was the end of it.

Hours later, I was seated on the bed. All dressed, I stared through the closed, glass window as the rain fell, reflecting on my mission as a waste and a failure. On The other hand, after seeing how much my mother was manipulated by a mad, malignant narcissist made me realize how much I needed to be careful of anyone, regardless of who, and listen very well to their use of words and any tone that sounded as if they were asserting some form of authority over me.

Soon after, his vehicle pulled up. After checking out of the hotel, I darted through the rain and into the front passenger seat of his vehicle. "Good night," I said. He replied but after we left the hotel parking lot, Instead of us going to visit my mother one final time, we made an immediate turn toward the airport which surprised me, and I asked, "We're not going back to the house first?" In his deep tone, he replied, "It's raining, and will take too much time." As mad as I was, I hid it very well through my silence. Instead, I shook my head and didn't care whether he saw me or not, then remained silent until we got to the airport. To think of why he couldn't just let me visit my paralyzed mother one final time before I left for the airport angered me very much. Out of the blue, he began to tell me about the good times he had with my mother during her healthy years. Again, this was all for me to leave with a good impression of him but it didn't interest me. Still up to that moment, he hadn't mentioned anything about how she became ill or how long she had been confined to her wheelchair.

He left after spending a few minutes with me at the airport. I called my mother, apologized for not coming to say a final goodbye, and reminded her that I would see her again, but didn't give her a time since the second visit was to be a surprise with other family members. As our conversation continued, she began to sob. I became silent for a moment, said goodbye, but couldn't hold back the tears.

CHAPTER EIGHT: FACING THE ORDEAL

I AWOKE IN NEW YORK CITY THE FOLLOWING MORNING UNDER A cloud of darkness, plagued by anger and resentment, in such a state of mind that I distrusted everyone except for close friends and family.

News had already reached the vicinity where my mother grew up on the Caribbean island of St. Vincent and the Grenadines that my mother was paralyzed and before you knew it, the phone was ringing nonstop by many who claimed to be family. Though many were only fishing for information so that they could start to fabricate the entire story, I was smart enough not to disclose too much information, and by doing so caused the rumors to spread even more. Some said that she was involved in a vehicle accident, while others said that she was found inside a nursing home. The worst story I heard was when a friend called to ask if it was true that she was found inside a homeless shelter. It brought tears to my eyes to see the distance that people would go to spread lies about a person who they had not even seen or knew anything about.

    I slid the window curtain open then with my arms folded, stared at the sunlit building across the street before I pulled myself together then walked my two cousins to the nearby school. Returning home was distressful since it was where all of the memories started. For relief, I spent a few hours at the famous Brooklyn Library situated at Grand army plaza, where I glanced at the pages of a few books concerning psychology. Upon ascending the exterior stairway, I was mesmerized by its beautiful, Egyptian-style architecture that decorated each side of the entrance. As you entered, you couldn't miss its wooden architecture with built-in fluorescent hanging from the ceiling, which left you wondering whether you were standing inside a museum or in a library. After making my way from floor to floor through various aisles, I grabbed three books and proceeded to a vacant table next to a massive glass window overlooking Flatbush Avenue. Glancing through each book very much enlightened me of how powerful words such as "I," "we," "can we," and "we want you to" are often used to influence a person. After reading how much a person can approach you with charm and generosity under the pretense of caring but in reality, their act is all to gather as much information as they can to use against you at a later date, trust issues were slowly developing inside me. Reading through those books reminded me of a relative who told me at a very young age that I should never, ever answer more questions than I'm being asked, never give more information than needed, and that not every question is asked out of curiosity. Many questions are asked to fish for information.

Everything was just too much for me to bear. I crossed the floor and stood before the massive glass window, and peered at the busy street below in a daze, curious as to what lied beyond. To ease my mind, I journeyed down the sidewalk where moving vehicles, the beautiful botanical garden and the surroundings all elated me. A calm sensation of serenity expanded my imagination beyond my expectations and prompted me to compose music like never before. After whistling and humming cheerfully to each new composition, they were unfortunately deleted from my memory due to the absence of a recording device.

A while into my walking, my stomach began to suddenly growl and caused me to stop. I took notice of the "Brooklyn College" sign, and realized that I had to walk a very far distance. "What time is it?" I asked a young lad. "A little after 12:30," she said in an African accent. I was shocked, not realizing that I had walked for almost two hours on a knee that wasn't quite healed, but it never affected me. On my way back, I came across a popular fast-food restaurant that I'd seen countless times on television and decided to get a fish sandwich. It was the most awful-tasting sandwich that I'd ever tasted. The fish was not seasoned and it was uncooked. Awfully looking liquid dripped from the inside of the fish each time the bun was squeezed. As I looked around, everyone seemed to be enjoying theirs. I dumped it into the nearby trash and continued on my way home with my stomach growling until I got to a three-way intersection and froze in my tracks without a sense of direction. Any wrong move would have sent me very much off the coast. I was just about to cross the street to ask a group of boys for directions when all at once, a familiar face of a young man was approaching me smiling. Before I could say anything, he called my name, and said, "Man, you haven't changed one bit." As soon as I recognized who he was, I said, "And neither have you. How long has it been, six, seven years?" I asked. "Going on to10. Man, time really flies," he said. Our conversation lasted for about five minutes. He expressed his sympathy for my mother, then we exchanged numbers and at the end of the conversation, he promised to assist in finding me a job. I told him that I'd be returning home soon. "Well, just in case, " he said, then went his way.

The following Sunday after church, I couldn't take it anymore as images of my mother ran across my mind continuously. I needed to talk to someone at the nearby precinct I'd seen earlier on. Knowing there wasn't anything they could have done, my hope was that someone there would have a friend or family member who was a senator, judge, Congressman or anyone else capable of doing a thorough investigation that may have brought charges against my mother's husband without her even having to say a word.

I made my way down the sidewalk through the unusually mild temperature beneath faint sunlight that was peeking through scattered clouds with my head tilted toward the ground, unaware of my surroundings. Just as I got to the precinct, with my eyes closed, I released a loud sigh, then entered the precinct clouded with cigarette smoke from a woman seated behind the counter with painted nails and a hairstyle similar to Tina Turner's. This was at a time when smoking was still allowed indoors, but to sit there without considering the discomfort of others being around smoke beats me. After placing the palm of my hand over my nose and mouth to prevent myself from suffocating, I approached her, confused as to whether she was a cop or not. Quietly standing at the brink of suffocation as cigarette smoke twirled into the air from every puff she took, I was very much expecting to be approached by a uniformed police officer until she suddenly asked, "What's up?" with a New York attitude that was fit enough for a television sitcom. As she knocked the cigarette inside an ashtray, I looked at her, still confused, and wasn't convinced that she was a police officer, so I never responded. Again she asked, "I say, what's up. You're here for a reason, right?" "Yeah, I'd like to speak to an officer," I said. "I'm sure I'm not a robot," she replied, then puffed the cigarette once more as smoke twirled into the air. After explaining everything to her, she informed me, because it all happened outside of their jurisdiction, there wasn't anything that could be done about it. It was something I knew, but just needed someone to talk to about it.

I left the precinct with my head hung like a lame duck and wandered into the nearby park occupied by several children and adults, and quietly sat on a bench, staring at the ground, very much oblivious to my surroundings.

After a moment, an unleashed poodle suddenly approached with its head bobbing continuously from left to right like a human rocking to a rhythm. Its tail was wagging vigorously in a playful mood, but I simply ignored him. He then moved to a new strategy by barking and leaping continuously, but was still ignored. A woman suddenly appeared, smiling as if we've known each other for decades and said, "He's only trying to make friends," but she too was ignored until she sat beside me. In a soft, compassionate tone she asked, "Are you ok, my child?" My eyebrows raised and for the first time, I lifted my head and looked at her with a fear that instantly made me uncomfortable. Something about her sounded so genuine that it arose my suspicion. "Was she in a cult searching for new members?" I asked myself, knowing how skillful they are in detecting a lonely or depressed person. "Is something wrong?" she asked, and I replied, "I'm fine." "I've been there and know when something's wrong," she continued. Concerned that telling her my problems could lead to the opportunity of her softening me into prolonging the conversation, I decided not to respond. In the most compassionate tone ever, she asked, "What's your name and where are you from?" Out of frustration, I angrily released a soft sigh beneath my breath and decided to give her a wrong name, "Nathan from St. Vincent and the Grenadines," knowing many were not too familiar with the name, and hoped that she'd end the conversation. To my surprise, she said, "Oh Nathan, It's beautiful. I've been to Canouan before." "Oh boy," I said under my breath with my head shaking. After hearing her constantly emphasizing the false name, which I knew she was going to use only for me to think that she cared, it really drew my attention on how susceptible I was to deception. It made me realize how much I could have easily been manipulated by anyone who told me exactly what I needed to hear at the moment. With no deterrence-based trust, I decided that it was time to end the conversation. "I have to go now," I said. "So soon, Nathan?" she asked. I replied, "Yep," and then was handed a card with only her name and telephone number. "No address?" I asked. after looking at the card. "Once we become familiar, Nathan, I'll make sure you get it," she said. Again, her constant use of the name Nathan meant that I wasn't going to allow her to lure me over to her place.

 The next day, I looked at the card, shook my head and tossed it aside, then purchased a calling card and called my mother, whose voice sounded shaky as if she was very tired and needed sleep. "Tired?" I asked. "I'm just putting some things together," she replied. We spoke for a few minutes before the conversation ended but in the back of my mind, something wasn't right. After I called a second time, a few hours later, the phone rang continuously, which caused me to believe that the number was once again changed. I became frustrated, and paced the floor restlessly with my head shaking. Not knowing if she was ok caused me anguish. Later that night, I tried to watch the basketball game but couldn't concentrate. After sitting at the dining table for a few minutes, the phone rang. "Out of state," I said to myself, which was obvious due to the sound of the telephone. I watched my aunt's husband pick the receiver up and said, "Hello," then paused a moment before raising his eyebrows in shock. "Is that my mother on the phone?" I wondered as I observed his body language. Finally, he hung the phone up, turned to me, and said "your mother is with your aunt." Many may think that at the moment, it should be a time for me to rejoice since it meant that my mother was now back with her relatives, but to us, it was a shock. I was utterly bewildered since we were all convinced that there had to be a reason for him to release her. Nothing made sense to me as I tried to figure out why my mother would be with my aunt who lived in a state that has one of the most brutal winters. The truth was finally revealed. Once you fall ill or disabled to a narcissist, you'll be tossed aside because that wasn't something that the narcissist signed up for. To them, you become a problem and will be considered to be nothing but an obstacle. They are ruthless, heartless, and selfish with absolutely no empathy toward others. They live in an imaginary world where they expect everything and everyone to be perfect. She was no longer of use to the narcissist. The truth about him had been now revealed, and it was now time to get rid of her by sending her back to us.

My aunt received a shocking call that night from officials at the airport who said that she had an emergency and needed to pick someone up. Although she was a medical personnel and dealt with ill people from time to time, this wasn't something she was prepared for that night. One look at my mother caused my aunt to burst her lungs out with a loud uncontrollable scream that attracted onlookers and airport officials. At first, she was confused as the airport officials led her over to my mom, who she obviously didn't recognize at first, then as everything came to her, she called my mother's name. My mother nodded "yes' ', then my aunt burst out screaming, and broke down. Many thought that I was exaggerating my mother's condition, but she had to be seen with their own eyes to get a sense of what I had described after I saw her that wednesday morning. The fact that the narcissist had all of our contacts during those years and never contacted any of us about my mother's condition proved how barbaric he really was.

From the very beginning, I knew that I was dealing with a narcissist, but to many, he was perceived to be a wonderful man as he constantly appeared at my mother's workplace even though she ignored him time after time. He found a way to convince her that he was a wonderful person, and the truth about him revealed that he was nothing but a brutal, sly, undercover monster who saw a weak woman from the very beginning. She was very vulnerable, which is a big advantage for a narcissist, especially one who is covert or malignant. First, they put you on a pedestal, mirror you and gain your confidence. Once they have achieved their goals and there's nothing left for them to drain, they'll quickly discard you and move on to someone else who will not be treated any differently. With absolutely no guilt, they'll fabricate stories about their innocent victims to feel good about themselves. Narcissists are all cowards who could never face you and accept their wrongdoings. Instead they rather find the easy way out by walking away without any form of explanation.

I needed to calm myself and decided to lie on the bed, but anger had the best of me. With my eyes staring ahead in despair, I was very determined to murder him, and I didn't care about the consequences.

The following morning, I awoke an angry man wishing that I had a brother, a gun, and a body bag to place the narcissist in. I reached for my wallet and realized that there wasn't even enough money inside of it to cover a taxi fare to the airport. Just as everyone left, I dialed his number. The number either rang constantly, was already changed or was disconnected. I was convinced that he had already moved. I shook my head, knowing that my mother was now in better hands.

After taking a moment to catch myself, I walked toward the window and quietly stared out into the gray hazy morning and imagined myself returning to St. Vincent. My mission was accomplished, and there wasn't anything else to prove, and I figured that it was now time for me to return, but my mother thought differently and wanted me to get an attorney.

Someone assigned me an attorney, and a few weeks after, on a brutally cold Saturday evening, I rushed out of the house to meet with him just before closing time, and found myself in the office of a different attorney. By racing out of the house, I forgot the assigned attorney's address behind, but was familiar with the area, and buzzed on the wrong bell since both buildings looked very much familiar. "Come in. Have a seat," the unassigned attorney said. His eyes were glued onto me, completely confused as to why I was there. I thought nothing of it since lawyers are swarmed with new clients very often. "Was I expecting you?" he asked, and I asked, "Mr. Jackson?" (which was not his real name). He replied, "No, but whatever you need to be done, I'm sure that I'll be able to help." "Oh, then I believe that this is an honest mistake, but thank you, anyway," I said, with a smiling face as I got back to my feet. On my way out, he said, "I can still help, you know." I replied, "Someone else is already familiar with my case, and it's a bit complicated." I exited as he yelled out, "Well, you know where to find me if you change your mind." I kept on moving with a smiling face..

    The exact building number for the assigned attorney wasn't something that I didn't remember but was confident that I'd recognize it. Making my way down the sidewalk as I scanned each building, in less than a minute, the building number appeared in front of me. After buzzing on the bell, I ascended a wooden stairway covered in red synthetic, plush carpet then appeared inside of an impressive waiting room decorated by plaques and photographs hung from the wall and a small table with neatly stacked magazines resting between an array of chairs. Not too far away was a young lady seated at a desk, typing away as the sound of her keyboard clattered the keys. "Good evening," I said, and she politely replied, "Good evening, Sir. Please have a seat, and I'll be with you shortly." "Thank you," I replied before I reached for a magazine from the center table. Five minutes into reading the magazine, she sucked her teeth. I glanced from the corner of my eye and saw her looking at her watch from time to time. Thinking that she wanted to leave I said, "Long day, huh," to which she shook her head and replied, "He needs to get off the phone. He's been with that person long enough." "Probably a client," I responded. "No, chatting with a friend," she said. After shrugging my shoulders with a smile, she sighed for a second time. Another five minutes went by and she pressed the intercom. The attorney yelled out, "Ahh, send him in. "Thank you," I said to the young lady with a smile, then entered the attorney's office where he reclined on his chair with both feet stretched onto his desk. Several framed certificates of achievements hung from the wall behind him. Next to them was a collection of books neatly organized beside a few photographs of him and others I assumed to be his attorney friends dressed in expensive suits.

Still deep in his phone conversation and without looking, he motioned me to sit on the chair at his desk that faced exactly where his feet were extended onto the desk, which would have placed my face in a position to look at the bottom of his shoes, something I considered to be a position of inferiority. Instead, I positioned the chair away from his feet, then sat with my face turned away as he continued his lengthy conversation that was beginning to annoy me. After about seven minutes, I sighed in frustration with my head shaking. He noticed, and ended the conversation. Without even offering an apology, he turned to me and asked, "Who are you?" I found the question to be quite rude. It could have been asked in a much professional way since he was an attorney. I looked him in the eyes and calmly answered, "The person you spoke with earlier today." "Oh, that's you. Mr. so-and-so already explained everything to me. No need to worry." The more he spoke, the more I found his attitude to be very much unprofessional. I found him to be quite pretentious with an appearance that was nothing less than a facade. Instantly my instinct told me to get up and leave, but he was already familiar with my case. "Maybe he was just a brilliant, honest attorney with a showoff attitude", I said to myself.. I decided to stop judging the book by its cover and give him the benefit of the doubt. Just as I decided to do so, he began to brag about all his accomplishments which didn't interest me, and I quickly switched the conversation to remind him that he was hired to do a job and that he wasn't my colleague. After a few minutes of small talk, a deposit was made and with that, we shook hands. For some reason, a feeling of uncertainty lingered over me on my way out and left me wondering if it was all a mistake of me hiring him.

As time went by, even though my mother was no longer with the narcissist, the memories of her seated inside her wheelchair kept flashing across my mind. Minute by minute, the question of me remaining in New York made me wonder if it was my worst decision ever. The cold, gloomy days left me in such distress that I couldn't even relate to many people properly. My brain had completely shut down, and it was as if English was a foreign language. There were times when I sat at the piano and happily played along to compositions by Beethoven and Mozart but at other times, considered them to be boring and found the piano to be nothing more than a useless, noisy instrument that was only occupying space. I'd leave the house and venture into dangerously unknown territories where residents stared at me and observed my every move, curious about my presence, but I had no fear and just needed to be alone. Many of my nights were spent quietly seated on a stone, heated in the lobby where I silently cried in isolation, but I displayed a smiling face to everyone who asked if I was ok. The moment I returned inside, the memories of my mother constantly flashed across my mind. My biggest challenge came at church where my only concentration was on the exceptional performance from the choir but after each performance, the massive crowd erupted into thunderous applause that instantly triggered my migraine. At the end of each service, everyone gathered at the entrance to introduce themselves, but I wanted no part of it. I trusted no one, had no desire to meet anyone and wanted to stay as far as possible from everyone unless you were family or a close friend. One Sunday, after getting to church late, every seat in the main sanctuary was occupied. On my way out, an usher approached me. "Come with me," he said. At first, I was hesitant before cautiously following him inside the lobby where I saw many viewing the service on several monitors mounted on the wall. There I found comfort from the crowd and from that day on, I decided that it was going to be my permanent seat. I began to purposely leave home late, hoping to get the opportunity to sit there where it was less noisy to prevent my migraine from triggering and from being introduced to anyone. The constant images of my mother's condition tormented me so much that at times it made me leave the service and wander the neighborhood to erase all the horrific memories, then go home with absolutely no desire for food. I had no appetite, and would force myself to eat, while silently contemplating my next move, which most times was hanging with former school friends who all lived about a mile away in different directions.

One afternoon, I decided to take the journey by foot. Upon reaching an area surrounded by abandoned houses, someone approached me from behind and shouted, "Hey, hey!" I stopped, turned, and saw a muscular-looking person whose face was cleanly shaved with a wig on their head. It was hard for me to determine whether it was a male or female. "Wanna have some fun?" they asked, unbuttoning their top, leaving their cleavage exposed. "What do you mean?" I asked, pretending to be dumb. The person pushed their tongue out, licked their lips up and down in a circulation motion. "No, thank you," I replied. "It doesn't cost much. Only five bucks," they continued. I replied, "It isn't my lifestyle." That statement sent them into a rage. "Who the (obscene language) do you think you are? Do you think you're better than me? You skinny (obscene language.) Do you know where you are?" I shot back, "No, tell me." "You're in East New York (obscene language) and I'll burst your behind." "Try me," I shot back. The person ripped their wig off and revealed himself as a bald male who continued ranting on. I was not scared and didn't move a muscle because at that time, I was at a point in my life where I thought that I had nothing to lose. After realizing how unsafe the area was, most of my Sunday evenings were spent at a park where a Caribbean football tournament took place but to me, it was a fashion runway and an auto show area more than it was a football tournament. Many came just to display their outfits and walked past you countless times to make sure that they were seen, while others stared at you in your face as they murmured. They made it their business to find out how certain individuals were able to obtain a visa to get to the U.S. Those who arrived in high-end vehicles parked them closest to the entrance to make sure they were seen, then bragged about their horse powers and how much the vehicles cost. When it was time for them to leave, they revved their engines the loudest to alert everyone that they were leaving. I needed to be somewhere else to ease my mind. One Sunday evening I was fortunate enough to come across a second park where children ran around freely, families and romantic couples gathered, and where basketball and netball games were played. It was where I found tranquility.

CHAPTER NINE: THE CHALLENGE

THE BRUTAL WINTER STOPPED. SPRING APPEARED, AND REVEALED a dazzled sunlight as the temperature climbed to above a comfortable 60 degrees and melted the snow. The once brown, barren trees bloomed with flowers and the famous Brooklyn Botanical Garden was transformed into a spectacular flower field.

Many who were trapped inside like bears hibernating for months finally came outdoors, and flocked streets, sidewalks, and playgrounds. Stores were occupied more and more and as business revenue increased, my friend fulfilled his promise by getting me a job. I showed up at his workplace the following day and found out that my job was to stand on a footstool for the entire day and scan the floor for shoplifters. The first thing that ran across my mind was my injured knee, which wasn't healed. On the other hand, I needed to complete

DOMESTIC DETENTION

the payment for the attorney service. I wasted no time and accepted the job, then hopped onto the footstool and casually scanned the floor. Nothing appeared unusual, even though it was my first time there, until a rugged-looking man with a scar below his eye and hair that looked as if it wasn't combed in months entered the store. Dressed in an oversized black jacket partly unzipped with an unidentified shiny object tucked inside his waist.. My heart almost burst through my shirt. I sighed, quickly looked away and pretended not to see him. The owner of the store, who was a man barely five feet tall, popped his head up from the office located at the back, and looked at me, then pointed toward the man. "This ought to be interesting," I said to myself, knowing for a fact that I was going to confront anyone whether they were armed or not. "Nope, nope, nope. It's not happening." I said to myself.

With my eyes kept on the man as he paced the floor from aisle to aisle, the owner kept his eyes on me, and I thought to myself, "Wait a minute, shouldn't this man be keeping his eyes on the man instead of keeping his eyes on me?" It was a behavior that showed me how far a person is willing to go to manipulate and instill fear inside of you to control you. It was as if he was trying to indicate to me that his presence meant authority. Pretending not to be looking at the man, I was under the impression that he was armed. Just as he looked in my direction, I looked away out of fear. It was as if he knew that the owner was about to sit at any minute because just as the owner sat, it appeared that the man quickly slipped something inside his jacket, zipped it up as quickly as he could, then walked toward me where I stood at the exit. Our eyes met. He then slid his jacket to one side, and it revealed the same shiny object I saw earlier on, which appeared to be a gun. Just then, the owner came forward and stood where the man was, and noticed something was missing. "Come here for a minute," he said, and I stepped down from the footstool and approached him. "Did you see him take anything?" he asked. I replied, "No." "Come with me," he said. After I followed him to the back where several boxes were piled everywhere, he said, "This job is too much for you to handle, so I'm sending you somewhere else where it's not as busy as here." Quietly, I released a sigh before I replied "Ok," but when I looked at the building number written on the address he handed to me, it appeared not to be too far from the number of the building that the South American girl gave to me a few months before I got to New York. Realizing how much she was willing to patch things up with her mother, on my way to my new job location, I scanned the buildings, then stopped at a particular building that very much convinced me that I was standing in the correct building. Even though I had lost the information she gave to me, it was as if I was looking at the paper inside of my hand. The numbers appeared to be in sequence. For example, if the number on the building was 1234, then the numbers written on the paper were either 4321, 1324 or 1432. But I just couldn't get over thinking that I was at the correct place. I exhaled loudly, shook my head, and decided that as soon as the time was right, I would take on mission number two.

As soon as I stepped through the door of the new job location, I was approached by the manager who was just about to exit with an unlit cigarette tucked into the corner of his mouth. Our eyes met, and he asked, "How may I help you, Sir?" I told him my name, and that I would be working there for the entire day. It was as if he almost went into shock. His eyes popped out, and the unlit cigarette fell from his mouth and hit the floor. He quickly picked it up then asked, "How come they sent you here?" "Less busy over here, I assumed", was my reply. The lady behind the cash register looked toward us, curious as to what was taking place. "What happened?" I asked the manager, but he never answered. Instead, he asked, "So you're going to be here for the entire day?" "Yeah, I just told you, and probably tomorrow as well." He went quiet for a second time with an uneasy look on his face before he walked over to the lady standing behind the cash register and said something. I hopped onto the footstool and watched as they whispered to each other before he returned, and asked, "So how long do you know your friend?" At that moment, I suspected that something was off. I replied, "Pretty much all my life." Then he continued, "So, you two are from the same island?" I replied, "Yes," and watched him walk back to the lady. I shook my head as I watched them whisper among themselves, and was under the suspicion that something dishonest was taking place.

Little by little, customers began to arrive. My eyes were on the manager as he greeted each customer with a friendly smile, while the lady behind the cash register glanced at me from time to time. Suddenly, a suspicious man and woman entered, each were pushing a shopping cart stuffed with emptied bags. My instinct told me that something was about to happen, based on the way they entered the store, glanced at me and quickly looked away without saying a word. Every other customer who entered the store greeted me, except for those two. The manager also pretended not to notice them as they made their way toward the back and disappeared out of view, but with a dome mirror just a few feet away from me, my eyes were kept on them.

Straight away, the manager approached. "Follow me," he said. I followed him into the disorganized basement where items in sealed and unsealed boxes scattered on the floor and on shelves. Some were filled, others were partially emptied. "Empty what's inside of the full boxes, and what's full, put them inside of the empty boxes," he said. Although to many it may not appear as anything suspicious, I knew it was his perfect way to keep me hidden from what was about to take place inside the store. I allowed him to carry on. Just after he left and before I started to unpack the items, footsteps were heard on the stairway. I looked, and recognized the shoes of the man who entered the store along with the manager. They were loading each stairway with boxes that were too heavy for me to move all by myself to prevent me from re-entering the first floor. Curious enough, I peeped through an open space between the stacked boxes, and saw the lady behind the cash register assisting the lady as they filled all the bags inside her shopping cart with items from inside the store. As much as I was tempted to yell out "Busted" just for fun, I smiled to myself as I shook my head. Half an hour later, the manager and the man cleared the stairway. He approached me and said that his reason for trapping me inside the basement was for him to create space on the floor to pack away items. To prevent myself from laughing, a nod from my head was just enough to respond to his foolishness. After having that experience, I wanted out immediately.

The clock was approaching 7 p.m. when I decided to approach the building where I thought the girl's mother lived. After searching for any name that was associated with the South American country where she was from, I came across a particular name and without wasting any time, hit the buzzer.

No one answered. Shortly after, a woman appeared from off the sidewalk with a shopping bag in her hands, and noticed me loitering. "May I help you?", she asked. I just want to see if someone is still living here." "Then, why not just buzz the bell?" she continued. I replied, "It doesn't seem to work." To prove that I wasn't lying, she pressed the bell, and for the second time, it never buzzed. After pausing for a moment, she said, "You know, I'm not supposed to be letting anyone in, but you don't seem to be the criminal type, so I'll let you in." Just for fun I said, "Actually, I've just been released after doing a five-year sentence for robbery." She opened her eyes wide in shock before she burst out, "What?!" I quickly said, "It's only a joke," before bursting out laughing. In a no nonsense mood, she asked, "Who are you looking for?". The girl had never given me a name for her mother, and having no idea what she looked like prevented me from responding. Suddenly, a lightbulb went off inside my head. Realizing that after a person reaches a certain age they no longer grow, I did a quick calculation in my head based on the girl's height, physique, and the length of time her mother was living in New York. I came up with an approximate height and description, called the name of the South American Country where they were from, and said she was anywhere from around 5'2" to 5'4" with long, black, Indian-type hair, about 160 pounds. Straight away the woman looked at me, and said, "Ohhhhh, I know who you're looking for, Check the last apartment to the back." My eyes instantly lit up and a smile appeared on my face, knowing that there was a second possibility of me reconciling a mother and daughter who haven't seen or spoken to each other in years.

As I entered the building and made my way down the corridor, my heart pounded against my chest. Memories of meeting my mother for the first time in almost 14 years flashed across my mind. A sudden tremble in my knee brought me to a halt. With my head rested against the wall, I struggled to catch myself before I released a loud puff of air. I proceeded before coming to a stop once more in front of an apartment entrance. My eyes were closed and I exhaled loudly for the second time, smiled to myself and was about to knock when suddenly, I stopped at the last moment. Something wasn't feeling right. I took a second deep breath then softly knocked on the door, but there wasn't any response. After a moment, I knocked for a second time just a little louder. In the same South American accent that the girl spoke with, a female asked, "Who is it?" My eyebrows rose and for a moment, I actually forgot my name. It took me a moment before I answered, "Me." "Me. Me who? Who is me?" she asked. It took me a second moment to catch myself before telling her my name and my reason for being there. Everything went so silent that you could have heard an ant walk. After about 20 seconds, I asked, "Are you there?" She never answered. Instead, the lock clicked, the safety chain rattled, then the door cracked open, and the lady pushed her head through the door. It was as if I was staring at the girl's double, which left me speechless. Soon after, she stepped out into the doorway and revealed her entire body. It was the exact weight and height that I had predicted. I said to myself, "Holy crap. I think I need to work for the FBI." I asked if she was the girl's mother. She never answered, then I asked for a second time, "Are you?" Then she asked, "Are you the one who got her pregnant?" "No, I'm just a friend," I replied. She continued, "But you don't sound as if you're from the same place as us." I replied, "No, I'm not, but I met her just a few months before becoming here. After hearing about her problems, I asked her for your information and told her that I was willing to help find you." She looked at me without saying a word, then I continued, "She was used by a man who knew that you were not around to protect her, not that I'm blaming you because your reason for coming here, I'm sure, was to make a better life for you and her. She realized how much she let you down and is willing to apologize." Her demeanor changed then as she softened and looked away with her eyes quietly stared at the floor. I continued, "Look, I'm still going through a worse situation after not seeing my mother for almost 14 years. Don't let this be you two. She wants you to meet your granddaughter." As I said that, her eyes became teary, then she said, "I'm a bit busy, and I need to get back inside." "Sure," I said and nodded, then watched as she re-entered the apartment, and closed the door behind her. I closed my eyes, took one deep breath then after I released, moved away from the door with my arms folded, then rested the back of my head against the wall where I almost shed a tear, knowing that I had just completed a second mission. A smile appeared on my face as I shook my head. Although I wasn't aware of her circumstances, it was now up to them to pursue a reconciliation. I held onto my perception and was somehow convinced that perhaps, she too was going through a rough time, had made a mistake by abandoning her only daughter, and was now living with the permanent guilt.

The following day, I showed up at my friend's workplace to thank him for all that he did but told him I couldn't continue due to the pain in my knee, which was true to a degree. The main problem was that I didn't want to be around the manager anymore. I didn't know who he was and wanted nothing to do with him, but didn't say anything to my friend. It wasn't my business and I thought that it was best to remain mute about everything since I wasn't sure what the manager was capable of doing to me. All I wanted was to stay as far as I could from him.

CHAPTER TEN: THE DECEIVER

Now without an income and no Plan B, the deadline for me to return to St. Vincent was approaching. As I was anticipating my return, I suddenly remembered that my documents were already with immigration. My brain went blank and I had completely forgotten about everything. I quickly called the attorney and asked if he could give me an approximate time as to when I'd be called, which he assured me was only a few months away. Still, in the back of my mind, there was just something about me not having much confidence in him. Maybe my case was just too much for him to handle or maybe, he was just a con artist, but I had a very low opinion of him and thought that he was very irresponsible.

As months went by, I began to wonder if remaining in New York City was one of the worst decisions that I had ever made. The cold and gloomy winter days robbed my happiness, and remaining at home only brought back memories of my mother. I cried in silence for absolutely no reason. To prevent myself from breaking down, I began to write music, and hoped that it would clear everything out of my head but found myself writing sad lyrics to my compositions. I needed to get the music out of my head as quickly as possible and began to look at the back cover of every pop record for any producer who worked on similar music that I was composing, but to get in touch with any of those producers was next to impossible. There were no telephone numbers or addresses listed on the back of the albums or cd's, and the few producers you got in touch with were only accepting solicited materials. Being unemployed and unable to afford an entertainment attorney put me back at square one with everything battling inside my head until one day, through hard work, I got in touch with a producer. After spending two weeks with him on the phone, we met inside his studio on a brutally cold winter night. Not knowing who he was, I looked around and saw photographs of him and many popular people I'd seen on television. The first thing I said to myself was, "Oh, no. Not again. Please don't tell me that this guy is another deceiver." Minutes later, I stepped up to the microphone and began to sing one of my songs. Just as I started, he stopped me. I thought something was wrong and looked at him, then he asked, "You're not singing reggae?" "No," I replied. He appeared a bit confused, but it didn't surprise me because for the weeks we'd been chatting on the phone without even asking, he assumed me to be a Jamaican who wanted him to produce my first reggae album. "Your accent is very thick for pop music," he said, and I replied, "Well, I've only been here for just a few months now." He folded his arms and stared ahead, quietly bobbing his head for a moment before he asked, "Who is your favorite singer?" "Nat King Cole," I replied. He was instantly taken aback because it wasn't something that he expected to hear. "I'm seeing more Michael Jackson, Prince, or a Babyface type singer in you. You already have the height and the build, but it's just the accent that I have a problem with," he continued. There was silence for a moment as he gazed at the floor, then suddenly said, "Why don't you sing something by Nat King Cole, exactly in the way Nat King Cole sang it in an American accent?" "Ok," I said, then stepped up to the microphone, took a deep breath, and in an American accent just like Nat King Cole, I sang "A cradle in Bethlehem." It marveled him and he looked at me completely baffled. Then said, "Sing something by Michael Jackson exactly the way Michael sang it." As I began to sing "Lady in My Life" he quietly looked at me with one arm folded and a finger over his lip, staring at me, while shaking his head. For a moment, I thought that he was disappointed, but then he broke into a smile and said, "That's it. That's your singing voice. Don't you ever change it because you were born to sing with that accent. It's authentic and unique and makes you stand out from the crowd. It will grab everyone's attention, whether they like you or not, and it's going to be very easy to market you singing this way." I thought to myself, "Just listen to this, nut. Why would I want to sing in an American accent?" Then I asked, "Do you seriously really want me to sing that way so the people who know me can laugh at me?" He looked at me just before saying, "The people who criticize you are always the ones who can't do anything for you. They are not going to take you to your destination, so do you prefer to listen to them or are you going to listen to me?" What he said stuck with me and within a few days, he was proven to be correct when I took a friend I grew up with to the studio. Thinking that introducing him to the producer was a great idea since he always wanted to do music as well, it turned out that it was not a very good idea. Just as I started to sing, he looked at me in the strangest possible way, then began to chuckle with the palm of his hand over his mouth to muffle the sound. The producer left the room and the first thing my friend said was, "Boy, what happened to people like you, eh? Why don't you sing with your real voice and stop fighting this whole music thing. You think you're Michael Jackson or something?" Then he burst out a loud laugh that he couldn't contain. I said nothing. Instead, I shook my head, knowing that he was the first person to prove the producer right. I just couldn't understand why someone would make a statement "that I'm fighting this music thing", when in fact, I'm from a family consisting of musicians. There I was doing my best to get involved in music, hoping that it would take all the pain away from what I was going through at the moment while trying to help him at the same time and there he was, trying to mentally assassinate me. From that moment, I continued to go to the studio all by myself. During that time, the producer introduced me to some very well-known artists, musicians, and a few actors who I thought I'd never have the opportunity to meet. What shocked me was to see how much smaller they all were in person. I looked at them and began to wonder how they could all sell so many albums and still end up broke. "Something has to be wrong," I said to myself. It wasn't until I began to spend every weekend at Barnes & Noble where I researched everything I could about the industry that I realized how easily it was for a singer, band, or group to become broke. The first thing that grabbed my attention was that 20% of your gross goes to your manager. Your agent gets another 10% and the producer gets 20% to 25%. You're still left to pay the record company their share, which could be as high as 82%, and that was all before you paid any taxes on everything you made. I learned that you may only make $10,000 from selling one million copies of an album, and you never get paid for a single because they are all used for promotional purposes. Whether you're the lead singer of a band or group, if you're not credited as a writer or a producer of that song, then you do not get any royalties. What scared me most was the publishing, which most people don't understand. Signing your publishing over to anyone is like giving away your entire retirement plan. The whole music industry business taught me that there isn't any friendship involved. It's all about business, and that the artists are always at the bottom of the pile.

For months, the producer tried as hard as he could to get me a recording contract, but record executives didn't want to take the chance. Two from separate companies stated that it was difficult to market me to a specific audience, which I thought was nothing but a foolish paradigm. Music is universal and regardless of who a singer is, their race or nationality doesn't matter. If a song has a beautiful or catchy melody, it will create a buzz, which is quite evident. Two examples are "Gangnam Style" and "Ameno." On the other hand, music began to change and signing an artist was more about image than talent. I wasn't willing to walk around wearing clothing three times my size looking like an inflated balloon with my pants falling from my waist exposing my behind. After working on six unsuccessful compositions with the producer, I thought that it was time to move on. As much as he was disappointed with my decision, music wasn't something that

I wanted to do anymore. We shook hands and ended on a high note, then went our separate ways. In 2012, he reached out to me and wanted us to work on a project that he was doing for an independent label, but I declined. The love that I once had for music had vanished, and to face an audience terrifies me. After the pandemic crippled the world in 2020 and I was locked inside, memories of my mother once again returned. To delete those memories, I decided to continue this book, which I started back around 2009. Out of stupidity, I was dumb enough to save it onto a flash drive and lost it all. Starting over was not an easy task. Forcing myself to relive the memories while drafting it together drove me insane. To ease myself, I reproduced a song and called it "Rendezvous Reboot" which was heard by British musician Oliver Sean. He was responsible for getting that song onto the iTunes top 40 charts. After that success, I worked on a song with him called "Waters," which was a song I was hesitant to release due to me not liking it at first. Fortunately, it went on to reach No.1 on the UK iTunes charts within days after its release.

My focus was now on the attorney who hadn't contacted me in months. I decided to reach out to him and for the second time, he assured me that everything was ok and that I didn't need to worry, but still, in the back of my head, something just didn't add up with this guy. How he spoke, folded his arms with his feet always extended on his desk, and whenever he was on his feet, he always talked about himself while adjusting his suspenders. Everything about him made me believe that he was more of a showoff than anything else.

Within a few weeks, someone got me a job as a messenger. I thought of my injured knee for a second time but realized that it was an opportunity for me to pay off the attorney's fee, and I had the chance to learn the city by foot. Most pickups and delivery schedules were done within 10 blocks, but anyone who walked over 10 blocks was compensated with cash or tokens that we then resold to the company.

As the autumn season began, just a few days of walking through Manhattan caused my knee to hurt. It was somewhat bearable, but was instantly swollen and felt as if it was frozen. No matter how many times I changed shoes, none were ever enough to cushion my knee. One day, I decided to rest inside a Barnes and Nobles bookstore and saw the woman I met inside the park with the poodle. I quickly darted between the aisles to get away from her. Fortunately for me, she was speaking to someone I say hello to in my neighborhood quite often. Just as she left, I approached the person and asked about her. His response was, "Stay as far away as possible as I can from that woman because she's a cult member from the Midwest, searching for new members." Without a doubt, I was convinced from the very beinning that she was scouting me out from the moment that I entered the park and realized that I wasn't ok, which is something cult members are experts at. The way in which she spoke in such a compassionate tone and the emphasis she placed on the false name I gave her made me realize that she wasn't a genuine person.

I got home that night tired with my knee hurting. After resting on the couch for about half an hour, a constant banging occurred on the door. I immediately peered through the peephole and saw three little girls, the oldest being about 10 years old, each with a bucket filled with candies in their hand. Hesitantly, I opened the door just enough with the safety chain still attached, then said, "Hey!" "Trick or treat," one replied. "Trick or treat," I said to myself, which was something that I'd only heard about on television. I had no idea that they were collecting candies. Suddenly, they pushed their baskets toward me. Thinking that it was an indication to grab a few candies, I opened the door, dipped both hands into all three buckets, grabbed a handful of candies and said, "Thank you," before I closed the door behind me. The next day at work everyone was eating candies, except me. Someone asked, "What's up, you don't eat candies?" I replied, "Yeah, but I had enough. A few kids came by last night and offered me some." He was taken aback and asked, "Wait, you're telling me that kids came by your house last night and offered you candies?" "Yeah they did. They pushed the basket toward me, said 'Trick or treat,' and I took as much as I wanted. I said thank you." He looked at me with his eyes widened in shock, then said, "No you didn't. Please tell me you didn't" before he busted out laughing. "Man, you just stole candies from the kids. What's wrong with you? You were supposed to give them candies, not steal their candies," he said. In a flash, I became the most hated man in America. I thought about the psychological effect it would have on them and purchased as many candies as I could, hoping that they'd return that night with their parents to scold me, but they never did.

By then, I was getting fed up with everything and needed a new path. A few people who knew about my situation suggested that I apply for a work permit, something that the attorney had never mentioned to me. After some research, I filled out an application, then found myself in line at the immigration office where I handed a woman behind the desk my application. "Good afternoon," I said as I slid my application toward her beneath the window. She reached for it, looked at it, then as she ran her fingers across the keyboard as it began to clatter she suddenly stopped and began to stare at the monitor while squinting her eyes. "Something wrong?" I asked myself. After a few seconds, she slammed the application back in my face and said, "Denied" without an explanation. With my eyes open in shock, I was baffled, and speechless. As I was about to question her, she motioned to the person behind me and shouted, "Next." Without saying another word. I sighed, shook my head, and exited the building, knowing that something had to be wrong.

Later that evening, I raced into the attorney's office and explained everything to him. To my surprise, his response was that I didn't need it and I shouldn't have applied for it. "Huh?!" Then how was I supposed to pay you if I didn't need to work, why?", "Because you don't need it." It was the most foolish statement I had ever heard coming from an attorney who was supposed to be helping me. Everyone in my position was told by their attorneys to do it, did it, and succeeded. Here was this man telling me that I didn't need it, then rudely asked if I'd completed my payment. "Yes," I replied. He pulled my files and scanned through everything and saw that I had already completed my payment, which was the very first thing I did before I started to spend any money on myself. In my head, I suspected that something was not right, so I asked, "Is there a problem with my application?" He replied, "There isn't," then reached for a paper from a drawer, quickly showed me with the word "Approved" largely printed on the paper as he stared at me to make sure that I saw the word. Before I could reach for the paper to examine it, he quickly slipped it back inside the drawer. I knew for a fact that it couldn't have been part of my files due to the fact and there wasn't any reason for him to keep that paper separate from my files. I said nothing, then decided to ask again, "But why shouldn't I apply?" Again he responded, "Because you're not supposed to." Everything about him took me back to the first time I entered his office, and I realized that my instinct was right about him all along. I was beginning to think that his expensive carpeted stairway, porch setting, and neatly organized books were all psychological eye-catchers since most people's impression of a person is mainly based upon their first encounter. There were question marks about him, but to research him was very much a challenge since Google was in its infant years. Most internet access was only at the workplace, and the only information I had on him came from my referral who was an honest person and was convinced that this attorney's credibility was superb based on the service he provided to a previous client. My instinct told me that there wasn't anything good about him. For him to tell me out of the blue that I didn't need it made me believe that something was wrong.

    I was now in a fight on my own but was determined to get to the bottom of it all. Month after month, I leaped out of bed at 3 a.m. to get to the immigration building by 4:30 A.M where I joined several people from all over the world. Some were from countries that I'd never heard about. We stood on piles of snow and ice with our frozen, ungloved hands tucked inside our jacket pockets and toes concealed in socks and boots that weren't designed to withstand the brutal winters. Buffs of stiff, icy wind rocked my shivering body back and forth as my teeth chattered uncontrollably only to then enter the warmth, congested building and be shouted at, and belittled by many who couldn't even properly pronounce a word in English. "Sit down, you sit down until I call you," one employee shouted from behind the counter, disrespectfully in a foreign accent to a lady who was almost twice her age. I shook my head in disbelief. A few minutes later, I approached a man behind the desk who checked my information and said, "Well, it looks as though everything is ok here as far as I can see." I took his word for it then left, confused. In the back of my mind, there still had to be a problem somewhere along the line. The quick glance that he took on the computer screen didn't assure me that everything was ok. With that information, and at the appropriate time, I applied for a second time. As I joined the line and made my way toward the glass window, I encountered the same lady who denied my previous application. There was tension as I approached, but I remained calm. "Good morning," I said with a smile, and this time she nodded with a stone face. I quietly sighed before sliding the application toward her, watched as she picked it up, then glanced back and forth from the monitor to the application. With my eyes closed, I released a quiet sigh once more beneath my breath. Just as I did, she slammed the application back into my face for a second time and burst out in a thick European accent, "Get a life. There is a list over there on the counter with the names of attorneys free of charge if you can't afford one." Her comment convinced me more than ever that the attorney was my roadblock. I raced over to his office that evening and saw that he was engaged in a phone conversation with the door widely open. After waving at him, he surprisingly ended the call and signaled me into his office. "Mr. ahhhh, what's your name again?" he asked as he rose to his feet, fiddled with his suspender hung from his shoulders. I reminded him my name, then he responded, "Yeah, that's right. I have so many things going on that I lose track of names sometimes. What can I do for you?" he asked.

Without any hesitation, I replied, "I was denied of my work permit for a second time." He looked at me shocked, paused, sighed before folding his arms, then shook his head without saying a word. "What exactly is going on?" I continued, and at that moment, he responded, "Nothing. That's why I told you not to apply." "Well, I'm determined to. I need to change my job" He looked at me, and with his voice slightly raised, said, "You're not supposed to." Again I asked, "But why? Everyone who is in my position was told by their attorneys to do it, did it, and got through. Why am I being told that I'm not supposed to?" He replied, "Just because everyone's doing it does not mean that you have to do it." "They're getting their advice from their attorneys." I shot back, and he burst out, "Their cases may be different." "Ok then, that's fine. Just tell me why I'm not supposed to. I'm only asking why. That's all." He ignored my question and I shook my head as he looked at me, then said, "Something's not right here, man, because I don't understand why you keep telling me not to apply." After making that statement, it was as if I insulted his intelligence. In a quiet rage with his eyes locked onto me, he exhaled loudly, then said, "You listen to me. I've been doing this for years and it's an insult to me whenever someone tells me that something is wrong with what I'm doing. Anytime I tell a person not to do something, it's because it's what's best for them." "No one's telling you what to do, sir. All I'm asking you is why, that's all," I said. He never replied. After he made the statement, "whenever I tell someone not to do something, it's because it's best for them," made me believe that I wasn't the only one who was having problems with him. The room suddenly went quiet for a moment and during that time, I watched him observe my body language and facial expression

DOMESTIC DETENTION

to see how much he could have broken me. We stared at each other for a moment, without saying a word before he asked, "Did you pay me everything?" I wanted to burst out on him, but instead, quietly replied, "Yeah, I told you that the last time when I was here. I can bring the receipts if you wish," but he never replied. Again, to me, something just wasn't right. It appears that his only concern was that he was compensated.

It was me against the world more and more each day. After finding my mother in the worst possible condition, I was told by the authorities that there was nothing that they could do. Then I came back to New York City and hired an attorney only to realize that he did nothing after paying him everything from my hard-earned minimum wage job where I had to walk the streets of Manhattan, carrying packages in my hands and over my back that was sometimes almost my body weight.

As I exited his office and made my way down the sidewalk, I met someone who knew about my situation and referred me to an attorney from St. Vincent. After meeting with that new attorney, he agreed to take my case and explained what I needed to do. The following night after work, I returned to the first attorney's office to retrieve my documents. Upon arriving on the sidewalk from across the street, I looked into his office, which appeared to be a bit dark with curtains drawn in front of a yellowish light and a silhouette of some sort. "Will he let me in at this time?" I asked myself before pressing on the buzzer. "Who is it?" he asked. I identified myself, but there wasn't any response. After lingering for about 40 frustrating seconds, shaking my head, sucking my teeth, and quietly cursing him from beneath my breath, the door finally buzzed. I ascended the stairway, shaking my head in disgust after realizing how much of a fake this man was, hiding his true colors and intentions among decent and hard-working Caribbean immigrants who probably thought that he was a gift from God. Unfortunately, he was from the same South American country that the girl and her mother were from, a country everyone in the Caribbean considered to be a part of the Caribbean. After getting to the second floor, I emerged into the waiting room, which was now unlit and was only recognizable by the light which came from his widely opened office door. "What in the world is that man doing alone here inside the dark?" I asked myself before I made my way inside his well-lit office where he was quietly seated behind his desk with his arms folded. "What now Mr......?" In a calm collected tone, I replied, "I just need my files." His eyebrows raised in shock, then he asked, "Can you come back tomorrow?" "My new attorney needs them now," I replied. "You hired a new attorney?", he asked. Yeah, I'm dissatisfied with the service you are providing me", I replied. His demeanor changed. He released a sigh and got to his feet in silence with a stone face. Like an old man slumping, he reached into the file cabinet and for the first time my eyes beheld my files. It looked unusually thin. Not many documents were inside of it. The first thing he pulled from it was the receipts. One by one he looked at them, then began to copy each document from inside of the file envelope. There was complete silence between us except for the machine whistling during every copy made and the paper rustling from every flip of his finger. After making the copies and without even placing them inside an envelope, he slapped the loose papers inside the palm of my hand. "Good luck," he said before walking away. I said nothing since I had already labeled him to be a covert narcissist, one who always turns into an overt narcissist after they've been exposed for their lies and dishonesty.

The next day, I handed my files over to my new attorney, who wasted no time in meticulously looking through every document, piece by piece. What he noticed right off the bat was that my case was incompleted. Important documents that were supposed to be submitted to the immigration from the very beginning of my case, were never submitted. That's when I realized that those missing documents were the reason why I was being denied a work permit each time I applied. I was angry at myself for not obeying my instinct one more time. The moment the first attorney showed me the false paper that read "approved", should have been the moment that I took my files away from him. I sat there in disbelief and felt like a fool as I tried to figure out how on earth can a human be that wicked and evil to know about a person's situation and still place a dagger inside their chest.

After my new attorney jumped on the case, everything was approved. As soon as I applied for my permit it was granted, along with a date for my interview.

CHAPTER ELEVEN:
THE AMERICAN DREAM

BEING IN AN APARTMENT ALONE WITHOUT A TELEVISION NEVER bothered me one bit. The computer I built from used parts was working fine, and to me, the internet, which was becoming popular in households, was more interesting than any television. My interaction with "islandmix", "go Jamaica" and "Radio Jamaica" kept my mind occupied from all of the hell that I was going through. My main objective was to keep moving forward in every way possible. I contemplated a lot on major investments, but after seeing how much I kept getting into problems after problems with many I trusted, keeping the majority of my hard-earned cash at home was my best option. Apart from starting a small investment and putting a few dollars into mutual funds, all of my cash remained at home tucked away in a safe place.

DOMESTIC DETENTION

One Saturday while doing house chores, my phone rang. As usual, I wasn't about to answer. Not answering my phone is something that I always do once I don't recognize a telephone number but since I didn't have caller ID, I thought that it could have been my new attorney so I answered. "Hello," I said, then heard, "Yoww," on the other end of the phone. I didn't recognize the caller, but the way he greeted me assured me that he was someone I knew. I asked, "Who is this?" and he laughed, "Ha, ha, ha guess who?" he asked. "I'm too busy to guess right now so if you can't tell me who you are, then I'll just end the conversation," I said. He laughed for a second time, then revealed himself as an old classmate who I hadn't seen since high school. We laughed and chatted for almost an hour, and decided to hang out the following day. I was a bit hesitant since I hadn't seen him for ages and knew that people change over the years. At first, I thought about meeting him at the mall, but the winter was brutal, and I decided to remain indoors and invited him to my apartment. The next day there was a pounding on my door. I looked through the peephole and saw a young lady standing there with what appeared to be a baby wrapped inside a blanket. Thinking to myself that maybe she had the wrong apartment, I asked "Who is it?" Before she could answer, my friend popped his head out from behind her with a grin on his face. I sighed then sucked my teeth with my head shaking in disappointment since I wasn't expecting anyone else to come along. As a child, I was taught never to show up at anyone's home unannounced and to never take anyone to a person's home unexpectedly. As they entered my apartment, my friend and I greeted each other with fist pumps. The young lady then said a quick, "Hi.", then instantaneously, her eyes were everywhere surveying the entire apartment as if she was looking for something that I was unaware of. It was pretty weird to me, but I said nothing. Suddenly, she asked, "Live alone?" "Yeah," I answered. "Your place looks very nice for a man," she said. I laughed and thought nothing of it. "You guys want something to drink? Remember I don't drink alcohol." I said. They burst out laughing, then I headed to the kitchen and returned with two glasses filled with ice, along with two drinks. The young lady's eyes were still all over the apartment. This meant to me that something was up. As my friend and I began to catch up on old times, she said, "Man, you need some company inside here. Being here alone doesn't get you bored?" "I don't mind being alone as long as my computer works. There's the internet and everything is peaceful. I love my peace," I replied. The conversation went on for another five minutes before she excused herself to the bathroom. Within that time the baby awoke, and being a lover of kids, I picked it up. I began to play with it while congratulating them on having a cute baby, and while doing so, the young lady returned from the bathroom, overheard me, and said. "Well, glad you love her because she needs a place to stay at the moment." Surprised by her statement, I looked at her with squinted eyes before handing the baby over to her, then sat just a few feet away from my friend, who shrugged his shoulders at me. "Why me?" I asked. "Someone told me that you were living alone and since we were all cool in school, I figured I'd ask you," he said. I sighed, then thought about it for a moment. As much as I wanted to say "No" since we hadn't seen each other in years, and didn't know if I could have trusted them, I had sympathy toward the baby and decided to get back to them within a couple of days. I had just started a part-time job that was one floor above my regular job but I had to leave home at 4 a.m. That concerned me since babies cry a lot, and could have deprived me of any sleep, which could have made me oblivious to my surroundings on a street that was occupied by just a few people each morning on my way to work. That fear came over me one morning after being misled by the clock and got the surprise of my life. The time had changed and not realizing it, I left the house an hour earlier and stepped onto the sidewalk, slipped my headphones over my ear, and kept the volume as low as possible as I normally did. After I glanced over both my shoulders one final time to make sure that I wasn't followed, I made my way down the sidewalk. The first sign out of the ordinary was that the corner store that was always open appeared closed. The few people I saw each morning on my way to work were nowhere to be seen, and the traffic light that was always about to turn yellow or red whenever I was almost at the intersection remained solid green. "Hmm, light stuck?" I thought to myself as I kept moving. After I cleared the corner, I looked one final time behind my shoulder and nothing seemed out of the ordinary. As I turned the corner and was making my way down the straight path toward the subway, a young man a bit shorter than I am and about twice my body size, who could have been identified by a scar on his forehead, popped out from nowhere like a magician. I jumped with my eyes widened in shock, then quickly calmed myself. "What's up?" he asked with his eyes locked onto me as my heart pounded. "Is this a robbery?" I asked myself, then calmly replied, "Nothing much. What's up with you?" He replied, "I'm trying to see if I can get a five off you," he said, and I thought to myself "What in the world is wrong with this guy?" I replied, "Unfortunately, I don't have that on me."

He took a pause, and looked at me before he said, "So, you're telling me that you walk here all by yourself every morning, and you don't even have $5 inside your wallet?" I was startled by his comment. It was the second time someone approached me that way, and asked for a five. I was beginning to think that anyone who asked for money always expected you to have money on you at all times. What struck me was when he said, "You walk here by yourself every morning." The fact that I had left home one hour earlier that day due to not setting my clock and he made that statement made me realize how much this guy had his eyes on me and probably never approached me because there were always people on the street. Not sure if he was armed or was about to overpower me, but I wasn't going to take any chances. I was already enrolled in a karate class and had no reason to hesitate from putting my skills to the test. After taking a deep breath, I stood in protective mode with one foot placed forward and my eyes locked onto him with the expectation of striking him directly in both eyes with two fingers. After that, I would have punched and elbowed him in the throat, stamped him as hard as possible on the side of his knee to knock him off balance, then kicked him where it hurts every man. After a few seconds, he walked away. I slowly backed between a few parked vehicles with my eyes locked onto him just in case I needed to cover myself from any gunshot but instead, he disappeared into thin air. From that day, I decided to change my route, which was a bit longer, but safety was the only thing I was concerned about.

Days went by as my friend and his girlfriend continued to bombard me with phone calls. Apart from other financial difficulties that they were going through, they stated that they needed to deposit at least 6 months' rent upfront for an apartment, which they didn't have, and I found it kind of odd but didn't question anything. The more I thought about the innocent baby who never asked to be in this world, I didn't even think twice. It was as if my brain went completely blank. I cleaned everything out of my savings, along with the money I was preparing to start an investment with and grabbed all the cash that I had at home, and handed everything over to them. Within a few weeks, they were inside their new apartment which was about a 10-minute drive away, but since it was still during the months of a brutal winter, I thought that the cold days had kept us apart. Little did I know that I was in for a big shock.

Not too long after, I was at the mall when a relative was desperately trying to add a young lady onto his cell phone plan but was having a difficult time doing so. The young lady was someone who I knew very well and was in the same position that I was once in. Since I had experienced it, I decided to help. At the end of the first month, I received the highest phone bill I'd ever seen. I wasted no time in contacting the phone company, which informed me that all the charges were due to the young lady making several phone calls to a certain Caribbean island throughout the day. At the time, cell phone plans were different. Only calls on weekends and after 7 p.m. were free, and that was excluding international calls. The young lady was out of touch with reality and had absolutely no idea how cell phone plans work. As much as I tried my best to explain to her, she accused me of adding all my charges onto her phone line and burst out at me in anger. "I don't see why my bill is so high, and yours isn't." In the calmest tone possible, I replied, "Well, that's because all my calls are made at night and on weekends, and I never use my cell phone to make international calls." "So, why can't I call during the day, eh? Shouldn't I be free to call whenever I want to?" she shot back. "Sure, you can, but your charges will be a lot higher," I replied. She shot back saying, "Well, no one's going to tell me when I should or when I shouldn't make a call." She continued to rant, and that's when I realized that I was in a lot of trouble. She decided to pay less than the total stated on the bill, and I was left to pay the remaining. I remained calm, even though the bill had put a serious dent in my pocket. It would have also cost me an arm and a leg to terminate the contract and disconnect the line. At that time, I wasn't aware of how credit worked and was worried about messing things up. Deciding to give her a second chance with the belief that she would have a conscience was one of the dumbest things I'd ever done. The next month's bill was almost doubled. With my arms folded and eyes and mouth widened in complete shock, I sighed with my head constantly shaking, then decided to call her. There wasn't any answer, and I left a message, "Hey, good evening. Kindly give me a call when you get this message. It looks like your bill has exceeded last month's bill." Within half an hour she called and just as I answered, she went off on me. "I just called the telephone company, and since I can't understand what they're talking about, I told them that I am not paying them because you and they have to be putting all these charges onto my phone. I don't trust you one bit." "Really?" I asked. "No, and I'm not going to sit back here and have you and the telephone company use me," she continued. "No one is using you. If you are constantly making international calls directly from a cell phone, don't you expect there will be a charge?" I shot back. She burst out, "What other phone do you want me to use?" "Just use a calling card for God's sake. They're everywhere," I shot back. She burst out, "What's the point in me using a calling card when I have a cell phone?" I once again shot back, "Because using the cell phone to call your country will only cause the bill to be higher." "Well, well, that's your business if you want to use them, but I am not using any, and you better find the money to pay this bill because you're a thief, and I am not paying a cent." I remained quiet as I shook my head in disbelief, knowing that I was dealing with another narcissist who refused to accept responsibility. Left responsible for two massive phone bills that could have been avoided, I had no choice but to disconnect her line.

My generous decision to assist those in need left me in a position where I was living from paycheck to paycheck. My only available money came from all the coins I saved from the change I received from purchases and from a habit of saving $10 in coins every two weeks, which I dumped inside a coin bottle after depositing my paycheck. Apart from that, everything else went to bills, and there was next to nothing inside my account. My refrigerator was empty, my cupboard was filled with noodles and for breakfast, the only thing I could have afforded was a butter roll that I consumed with iced tea from the kitchen at my workplace. For lunch, I had noodles and the cheapest juice I could afford, which I diluted with water and sugar. It didn't take long for everything to affect me one day on my way home. I was seated on the train one night when there was a sudden pain in my stomach that caused me to crouch inside my seat for the entire trip. Just as the train reached my stop, I attempted to stand but the pain worsened. Still, in a crouching position, I staggered off the train, then stepped inside the apartment when in an instant my mouth was quickly filled with excessive saliva. I raced inside the bathroom and placed my face over the bathtub, but nothing happened. The pain was so intense that it prevented me from standing. After crawling my way out of the bathroom, I coiled onto the living room floor and was completely passed out until the following morning at around 8 a.m. as the pain continued. My short time on the job meant that I was still on probation and didn't have health coverage. With such extreme pain, I had no choice but to quickly hop into a taxi to the hospital. As soon as the lady approached me, the first question she asked was "Do you have insurance?" "Huh? I'm feeling ill, and I don't have any. Whatever you do, just send me a bill. I'll pay for it," I said. To me, it appeared as if it was her first day on the job, or perhaps, her mental state was in another world. She looked at me as if I was from another planet, then said, "I'll be back," and walked away. With my hand still pressed against my tummy, I groaned like a kid. After waiting for about 15 minutes, a droopy-looking doctor who appeared as though he hadn't slept in days appeared. Just to wake him out of his slumber for fun, I wanted to ask, "What's up, doc?" but thought that he might not have had a sense of humor. "How are you," he asked, and I replied, "I've been having this stomach pain since last night," as I rubbed the area continuously with the palm of my hand. "Turn on your side," he said and slipped his hands into a pair of gloves. He massaged my side with the palm of his hand. "Does it hurt?" he asked. "No," I replied. "Turn on your back," he said. I turned and he continued to massage my stomach. "Nothing hurts?" he asked. "No," I replied, then he insisted that I completely change my diet and refrain from eating and drinking certain food. He handed me a written prescription for an over-the-counter medication that worked within a few days.

Apart from a hefty phone bill, I realized that I would be receiving a hospital bill and was in desperate need of cash. I reached out to my friend who borrowed the money and just as the phone rang, he picked up. "What's up?" he asked in a jovial manner, and I asked, "What's going on?" "Just surviving," he said. Before I could say another word, he began to whine about how bad things were with him and his girlfriend, and that I needed to call him back in a couple of days. As badly as I needed the cash, waiting two weeks wasn't a bad time, in my opinion. In my head, I somehow believed that it was all a game. I shook my head in disbelief and thought of how dumb I possibly was delaying my investment, drying up my savings, and handing over my emergency cash to assist a person I hadn't seen in almost 10 years and another person whom I knew absolutely nothing about. To justify not looking like a fool, I chose to think about the innocent baby.

Almost two weeks after I checked the mailbox, the first thing my eyes saw was a large brown envelope with no return address wrapped with a rubberband around a small envelope that was from the hospital. As much as the large, brown envelope stimulated my curiosity, it was the small envelope from the hospital that interested me more. Eager to see the total on the bill, I opened the envelope and was blown away after seeing how much the hospital charged me for less than two minutes of service. "What in the world?" I asked myself, then called the number listed. The lady informed me that it was due to me not having any insurance. "For two minutes?" I asked. "I'm sorry," she replied, then I asked, "So, there's no way this can be reduced?" "I'm afraid not, and you will also be receiving a bill from the doctor as well," she continued. I sighed and shook my head, then jokingly said, "Well, it seems like I might just have to marry a nurse to settle this. You wanna marry me? I'm a Caribbean man who can cook, you know." She burst out laughing, and I continued, "I don't have a ring at the moment, but I noticed a soda machine at the hospital, so we can always grab one from a can. What's your favorite soda?" For the second time, she burst out laughing, then said, "Sorry, sir, but I'm taken." "Ok," I replied, then ended the conversation.

All my focus was then on the large envelope. As I opened it, I was shocked to realize the date for my scheduled interview with immigration was less than 90 days away. "Wow," I said to myself, realizing how much shorter it would have been if the first attorney hadn't scammed me. I reclined onto the chair with my eyes closed, then released a loud sigh, and said, "Thank you, God." Then, as I continued to read, I noticed that it stated that I may need to pay a fee that I sure didn't have. The next day was Thanksgiving and as much as I didn't want to call my friend, I figured that the two weeks had already passed and I needed to give him a call. The phone rang out for every attempt made, then after the 6th or 7th attempt that day, he answered. "What's up?" I said. "Ummm, you tell me. We're busy at the moment. As a matter of fact, we have a few people over," he said with an attitude, which to me was an indication that I was interrupting his day, but I didn't care and continued. "I'm in a jam at the moment, and would like at least $300." I said. "I don't have anything," he responded, and I replied, "You said two weeks, and I gave you more than two weeks." "Come on, man, you're acting as if I'm not going to repay you," he said. "Oh, I'm not thinking that at all. All I asked for is 300 dollars," I said. "But you've been calling constantly," he said. With that comment, I took offense and replied, "That's because no one answered. How much can you give at the moment? Ah mean, we're talking thousands of dollars here". By asking that question, his nice boy attitude changed into a thug, and he burst out, "This is explicit Thanksgiving, man." In a calm tone I responded, "But I could have been calling you to say a Happy Thanksgiving." He never responded. Suddenly, his girlfriend came on the line, "But your purpose for calling was not to wish us a happy Thanksgiving." I was a bit surprised to hear her voice. This was a woman from another island who I had only recently met through him. Hearing her make the statement, made me ask, "How many times did you all call me when you needed my help?" She burst out, "So that's what you do? Help people, then talk about it?" "Huh?! What in the world are you talking about?" I asked, and she shot back, "If you had told him "no" the first time like everyone else, then he wouldn't have called you back." Her statement caught me by surprise, then she unexpectedly burst out, "You know what, man, to hell with you, and please don't call here with your nonsense. Nobody forced you to lend us anything, you chose to. If we ever need help, we will ask someone else." I was furious, and shot back at her, "So you can do the same thing to them as you did to me?" My comment angered her, and she burst out, "Man, eff you, and go (expletive) your mother." With that, she slammed the phone in my ear and left me with my mouth open in complete shock. The same people who came to my apartment, and pleaded on the phone day after day for my assistance, no longer needed me. I was now their biggest enemy, and once again, had lost confidence in everyone. With my head shaking, I found a seat on the same chair where she and her boyfriend sat and thought of how stupid I was, always going the distance mile for many who are yet to walk an inch for me. After becoming distraught, I needed to be alone. I called my aunt and told her that it was impossible for me to make it to her house for Thanksgiving after I'd already assured her just a couple of days before that I would. It was now up to me to prepare myself a Thanksgiving dinner. I took a walk to the bank and attempted to make a withdrawal, but instead of cash dispensing, a receipt came out with the embarrassing words "Insufficient funds." With my head hung to the ground, I returned home and looked inside my refrigerator, which I knew was empty. Somehow I expected to see food magically appear and when it didn't, I reached for a cup of noodles from the cupboard. I emptied it into boiling water, dished it out, then sprawled onto the rug, and stared at the ceiling as the stream rose and the aroma filled the room. Later that night, I awoke at the same spot under darkness with the palm of my hands locked behind my head with my eyes once again glued to the ceiling. Even though I was distraught, the serenity transitioned into the best sleep that I had experienced in months.

The following morning, my attention went toward the immigration letter, and realized that I needed some information that I thought would have been easily accessible. It turned out to be much more difficult. Each night I found myself on my knees in complete darkness, crying out to God. The more I did, the more my knee pained. Lying in bed night after night was my only option as the warm tears streamed continuously down my face, and soaked both sides of my pillows. "Why me, God?" I'd ask. Then the scriptures that stated, "He who began a good work in you will complete it to the end," and that "He will never leave you or forsake you," crossed my mind. At the time, they weren't comforting words. I felt as though I was abandoned, and began to lose all confidence in God, and thought that He wasn't as powerful as everyone made Him out to be. "Why would such a loving, and powerful God allow something like this to happen to me after helping people by putting them first and by making their lives easier while my life became harder," I asked myself. The more I doubted His ability, the more I found myself crying out to Him. Then one night while praying, I swiped my fingers across my cheeks to wipe the tears away as I normally did. This time all I felt were dried remnants of tears. They were pretty much uncomfortable as if my eyes were filled with gravel. After looking inside the mirror with the expectation of seeing loose eyelashes stuck to my eyeballs, there weren't any. The following morning at work, after washing my eyes constantly throughout the day with eye wash, the discomfort continued. I raced to a nearby optometrist without an appointment, and the receptionist refused to allow me to see the doctor because I was still without health insurance. Leaving was not my option. I demanded to see the doctor. After a phone call, she handed me a form attached to a clipped board which I filled out. I agreed to be responsible for all expenses, then handed it back to her and quietly sat for almost two hours before the optometrist decided to examine my eyes. A prescription that cost an arm and a leg was given to me, but weeks after using it, the discomfort continued. A second doctor was my second option, he prescribed a second eyedrop that was much more expensive than the first, but the problem continued. Annoyed and broke, I decided to see a third doctor. He instructed me to purchase a particular $10 eye drop from over the counter. At first, I thought he was crazy since the two other eye drops cost me everything. After purchasing the $10.00 eye drops and within a few hours of using it my eyes got the relief needed.

Week after week I was taking coins from my coin bottle and was dumping them into a machine for cash at a bank close to my workplace. One day on my way to the bank with my $200 worth of coins spread loosely inside my bag, I was approaching the intersection when the walk sign began to countdown toward zero. Thinking that I could have beaten the light, I took off and successfully made it across the street, then the strap of my bag burst. Almost all the coins fell from my bag and rolled inside the drainage. I screamed in frustration and shook my head in disbelief after I was only left with almost $40 worth of coins.

Even though cashing in my coins was a big help, I was still in a financial dilemma and had no choice but to contact a particular company and ask if they were willing to lower the monthly payment on a bill. They agreed, but within the second or third month, even though I had fulfilled my promise, there were serious discrepancies after a man called from a collection agency and threatened to body slam me to the pavement. He claimed that I hadn't paid anything in months, when in fact I never missed a payment. "Huh?" I said on the phone as I tried to explain that there had to be a misunderstanding. He still wasn't having it, and kept on ranting, "Pay me my money," he shouted. I was very much unaware of who the individual was since I'm never the type to borrow money from anyone. At first, I thought it was a joke, and asked, "Pay you your money? What are you talking about? Who is this?" He identified himself as an employee of a collection agency. I was still confused as to why he'd called me. "You owe me," he continued. "I have no idea what you're talking about, and I do not owe you." "Yes you do, yes you do. I'm fed up with people like you who never want to pay your bills." "What in the world are you talking about?" I shot back. "If people who owe us more than you do, are paying, so can you. Pay me my money". He continued to rant. "Calm yourself down. I can fax you all the receipts if you need me to, so stop acting like you're powerful from behind that four-by-four cubicle." Then he snapped, "You better not tick me off right about now before I come there and body slam your behind," and I shot back, "Bring it on! I'm from the Caribbean and believe me when I tell you that I will blaze you with bottles and stones like missiles. Believe me when I tell you that I won't miss." We went back and forth for almost five minutes until I decided to slam the phone in his ear.

The way I hit rock bottom all because of my generosity toward the needy, taught me a valuable lesson. To some people I was UNICEF. To others, I was either the Salvation Army or the sole proprietor of a charity. Even though I was facing my ordeal, many were in much more difficult, and painful situations than what I was faced with. I felt their pain and had compassion toward them. My heart was softened, and I placed myself in their position and decided to assist. The fact that those same people turned out to be ungrateful toward me, showed me how far a person will go to push you into the dirt to pull themselves out of the mud to achieve anything that they want, even if it means sucking you dry of everything at your expense. I just couldn't say the word "no" to anyone. After one problem was another. Everything was just going against me. Many who I thought were my friends, were only trying to get as much information as possible from me so that they could have used it against me and stab me in the back. I couldn't believe it when someone called back to St. Vincent and exaggerated a story about how terrible my life was and that I needed to return home. They even went as far as to fabricate an entire story about how my mother was now in a much better position than the one in which I was. This was a person who was arrested numerous times. One was for such a nasty crime that surprised many except me because I already knew he was a scumbag who was constantly looking to see who was his next victim.

    Putting everything behind me was very much difficult in a city where many appeared angry. I wasn't sure if their behavior was due to financial strain or any other pressure, but it was just a complete shock to see the way many behaved as if they needed anger management. From the streets to the buses to the subways. People burst out on you for the simplest reason, such as walking too close, accidentally bumping into them, or looking at them because their faces may look familiar. If you were vulnerable, quiet, appeared nonviolent, or never put a stop to their attitude, you were their target. They'd jump in your face and burst out on you for the simple fact of being ignorant about something that they can nicely speak to you about. One such person was a supervisor at a messenger company where I worked. He was a man who was easily angered by everything, and being around him was like mental torture. This was a man who went off on almost everyone for the simplest reason. Losing a bet on his sports team transformed him into a madman. He knocked packages about everywhere, slammed phones in everyone's ears, and spoke to grown men as if they were children. Since I was seated not too far away from him, I was faced with a daily dose of his wrath. I became so fed up and wanted out that one day on my lunch break, I approached a large map of the United States pinned onto a wall. I closed my eyes and then pointed my finger on the map. It landed in Wilmington, Delaware, and I said to myself, "Perfect." I had nothing going for me except the memories of my mother's condition twirling inside my head. I figured not having a wife or any kids meant that it was the perfect place for me to isolate myself from the world. At the time, I was apathetic at a point where I felt, "It is what it is. Whatever happens, happens." My mission was already completed and that was enough. I had absolutely nothing more to lose. If I needed to return to St. Vincent, and the Grenadines then so be it. I'd go and just isolate myself from everyone except family and close friends.

A Jamaican coworker who had seen enough of the way he spoke to me approached me. "Brethren, mek I tell you something, Nobody feh talk to you like that, man. You need to put a stop to it cause if yuh na stop him, him ah go continue," He said. "Let him release his anger because he needs to release it," I replied. He looked at me, laughed then said, "Release anger pon you! Brethren ah wey wrong wid yuh man? Eh, yuh mad?" Before I could say another word, he walked over to the supervisor and said something. To this day, I still don't have a clue as to what was said but after that, the supervisor calmed himself down for a little bit. The fact that I wasn't arguing with anyone convinced them that I was soft but the reality was, with the anger of my mother's mistreatment still stirring inside me, I was a silent ticking time bomb ready to explode at any moment. I had learned from an early age how to control my anger, and that was to my advantage. Still, I couldn't understand how people can burst out on you for the first time about something that they can just speak to you nicely about. I can understand someone getting angry about something they've spoken to you about dozens of times, but to burst out like that told a lot about who he was and how much anger he had inside him.

I was still wondering if God had abandoned me and if my prayers had fallen on deaf ears. Once again, I found myself crying out to Him. Just before my interview, all the documents except one were missing. It was still a bit of a relief, knowing that a weight had been lifted from off my shoulder. I smiled, then shook my head after realizing that the same God who I thought had abandoned me had just proven to me that He never did, never will, always shows up at the exact time and that He knows best.

The night before my interview, I was lying in bed with the bedroom door widely open and was quietly staring straight ahead when everything flashed across my mind. The pain, tears, discomfort, and discouragement from the many who encouraged me to return home. Tears flowed down my cheeks like a fountain and as much as my eyes were red and swollen, I let it all out.

The following morning, I awoke early, exited the bedroom, then stared out into the gray, gloomy morning before I reached for the manila envelope filled with my documents, except for one piece that tried to deceive me to remain at home. After pacing the floor back and forth with my arms folded. I reminded myself of the scripture stated, "He who began a good work will carry it on in completion." I wasn't sure how it was interpreted, but it was enough to make me fall onto my knees and cry out to God one final time. Tears streamed uncontrollably down my cheeks then without warning, a migraine triggered. I became so dizzy that I had to creep like a baby toward the couch. With the palm of one hand cushioned behind my head and the other palm resting on my forehead, I quietly groaned with my mouth open. Two hours later, I made it to my feet, prepared myself, then staggered out of the apartment like an intoxicated man. Moments later, I was wedged between two people 20 inches apart, reclined on the train with my eyes closed, only to be disturbed by the rattling sound of the engine and the annoying, squeaky sound from the wheels as we turned the corners. I began to daydream about career paths and the first thing that crossed my mind was to become an immigration attorney. After stepping onto the rough rocky roads filled with hurdles and obstacles that I had to push aside to clear my path, to me it was best to assist those who fall on the same path in which I trod. But countless hours locked inside an office wasn't going to expand my imagination enough. Being a pilot wasn't much different, even though it was my childhood dream. The hours crammed inside a cockpit smaller than any cubicle at 30,000 feet would have driven me crazy, and I had lost all interest in music since everything had changed from talent to image.

Suddenly, there was a long continuous squeaky sound as the train came to a stop at my final destination. I quietly sighed and got to my feet with my heart thumping continuously against my shirt. My migraine was of no distraction. 10 minutes later, I found myself seated in a packed open room with dozens of people from all parts of the globe. Some were seated quietly chatting and murmuring in numerous languages that left me curious as to what was being said. Others sat in silent contemplation with their arms folded, and were staring toward the floor, stupefied as they awaited their fate.

About an hour later, a petite woman less than five feet tall appeared inside the doorway. Her eyes squinted at the paper in her hand as she whispered a name that everyone found difficult to pronounce. She walked around the room, dropped her hands to her side in frustration, then called the name for the second time. As I watched her lip movement, I was convinced that she was calling my name. "Right here," I yelled, with one hand shot through the air like a student in a classroom. I sprang to my feet in an instant, the envelope that was resting on my lap opened and fell. Everything littered the floor. "Coming," I yelled out, quickly as I heaped the documents in a rush which caused many to mumble and awkwardly stare. "You mean to tell me that him nah know him name," one woman from a particular Caribbean island whispered in her dialect. "Now he gwine and mek the woman get angry, then tek it out pan somebody else now," the woman seated beside her who was from a different Caribbean island murmured back to her in dialect. I simply ignored them and met the lady inside the corridor. Her eyes were fixed on me in the most intimidating stare ever. Just as I reached her, she shouted, "Didn't you hear me calling your name?" "No I didn't," I replied in a very polite manner. "Then you better have everything," she angrily replied. No response came from me and she shouted for a second time, "I'm talking to you." This time I replied, "Almost all of it." "This way," she said. As we walked side by side down a wide open corridor and my heart pounded against my chest, she unexpectedly turned toward me and gave me the warmest smile ever, then softened. "No need to panic," she said, which caught me so off guard that I couldn't even return a smile. Shocked by the comment, I pinched myself to make sure that I wasn't hallucinating. The same woman who was harsh to me a few seconds ago had transformed into a generous, polite person.

A photograph of a young man dressed in a foreign army suit resting on her desk caught my attention as we entered her office, and I asked, "Your son?" She nodded. "Yes. He's my everything," she said. It was another clear indication that there truly is a special bond between a mother and her son. After laying my documents before her on the desk, I watched her scrutinize each one. As she looked through the pages of my passport, she quietly said to me, "You've been here for a long time," and I nodded. Then like a mother to a son, she said, "I can tell that you've been through a lot." I responded, "Yes," and couldn't prevent the tears from streaming down my cheeks. "Sorry," I said. "It's ok, you can let it out," she said before she handed me a tissue she pulled from a box. As I wiped my eyes with the tissue, everything took me back to the day when I found my mother. There was silence for a few seconds as she stared at me, then looked at the photograph of her son for a moment, shook her head, looked back at me, and said, "Sorry about everything." What she said touched me. There I was with a petite woman who first appeared tough but was as gentle as a baby and understood me in a way that any genuine human being would. She sighed and quietly said, "I know it's a bit difficult, but you're going to have to bring one more document. As soon as you get that, everything will be ok for you." I nodded, "Yes," and then she continued. "Are you sure you'll be able to get it?" I replied "Yeah." She gave me a specific date to return, but the time she gave me baffled me because it was very close to her office closing time. Nevertheless, I wasn't going to let it stop me.

Within a few days, the document was inside my hand. Not a time was wasted until the train was delayed for unknown reasons. With an hour and a half to spare, the station manager's voice blared over the intercom that all trains were delayed by 30 minutes. "What!" I said to myself with my eyebrows raised in shock. Racing to a second train would have only put me much further away and on the other side of town. As the tension built up inside me, I leaned against the platform post with my head shaking in frustration, then paced the floor to calm myself. Suddenly, two headlamps beamed from around the tunnel. The massive 85,000-pound train came into view and barrelled around the corner, then squeaked to a complete stop. I waited patiently as passengers exited, then darted my way onto the crowded train with the expectation of it moving in seconds. After 10 minutes, we were still at the station without any explanation. Agitated passengers began to murmur, sucked their teeth, and loudly vented their anger. "Come on, man," one man shouted, then another shouted, "This is ridiculous." By then, my 30-minute head start had dwindled to less than an hour. As much as I was tempted to race off the train, hopping onto a second train would have only placed me much further away and across town. Hopping onto a taxi was my second choice but the $10 inside my pocket wasn't going to cover the cost of the journey. Suddenly the doors closed and the train crawled out of the station and into the next, then stopped several feet away before it reached the platform. Passengers noticed and continued to vent their frustration as I quietly stood with my eyes closed and teeth sucked with my head shaking. Another 10 minutes later, we crawled into the station of my intended stop. I raced off and leaped onto the escalator, and hopped over every other tread until I exited the subway and appeared on the sidewalk where flurries gently fell to the ground before they evaporated.

My heart pounded with every step I took as I raced down the sidewalk. I got to the building and met a lone security guard pacing the floor back and forth. The look on his face indicated that he was stunned to see me, then he looked at his watch. "Man, you're very late. Go, go, go, go before the building closes," he said. I raced into the building and was stopped by a second security guard who quickly scanned me, then waved me through.

As the elevator shot up to the floor, with my eyes closed I released a sigh, then just as it stopped, stepped off, then entered the same open room that was packed with many just a few days prior, only to notice that the only person there at that time was a female security guard who was glancing at her watch as if she was patiently awaiting to leave. "Make it quick. Run, man," she said in a Caribbean accent. I raced over to the counter where I met a lady and informed her about the specific agent I needed to see. "Hold on," she said before she disappeared into a backroom. Two minutes later, the agent arrived and looked at me as if she was confused, then glanced at her watch. I was scared for a moment, thinking that she had already forgotten who I was, then gradually a smile appeared on her face as she slowly bobbed her head and said, "Give everything to me." After handing everything over to her, she disappeared into the back room. There was still a sensation of nervousness as I waited for her return. About ten minutes later, the door opened and my heart pounded as I watched her walk toward me with a smile on her face. She handed me my passport with one hand and saluted me with the other hand, then said, "Feel free to visit your family whenever you wish. I know it's been a long time." I saluted her back, and said, "I sure will. Thank you very much." She smiled at me one final time, then disappeared into the back room. I released a loud sigh that caught the attention of the female security guard who said, "Boy, I know how it feels." I shook my head and calmly exited the building without saying a word before then stepped onto the platform as the snow continued to gently hit the ground and evaporate. With my hands tucked inside my pants pocket and my head leaned, I stared at the exact spot where I stood in the wee hours of the morning, year after year in frigid temperature as my toes and fingers burnt and as the memories returned, the tears began to flow down my cheeks.

The first thing I did as soon as I entered my apartment was fall on my knees and thank God for never leaving me, even though I had doubts. I felt the warm tears stream down my cheeks and this time, for some strange reason, I couldn't contain myself. I screamed, "Thank you," expecting to hear Him reply, "You're welcome." His silence and presence through it all were enough to convince me that He had fulfilled his promise.

After taking a shower, I wasted no time sliding beneath the blanket. With my eyes closed, everything replayed inside my head, the awkward handwritten letters, the attorney who swindled me, and those who turned their backs on me after I helped them. Twenty minutes later, I was on the verge of dozing when unexpectedly, I was jolted by the blast of a powerful bass speaker from the apartment above. The ceiling rattled. It was as if a force of something gushed to my head and triggered a migraine without any warning. My brain pounded against my skull, and I grabbed onto my forehead, rolled from side to side then took a deep breath to calm myself down to prevent a brain explosion. "You gotta be kidding me," I said to myself with the palm of my hand resting on my forehead. I exited the bedroom and closed the door behind me. As I headed toward the kitchen, the thumping sound of footsteps down the stair grabbed my attention. I looked through the peephole and saw the 14-year-old girl who lived in the apartment above me racing down the stairway. Immediately, I cracked the door open with the safety chain still attached and politely asked, "Is it possible for you to just keep the music down, please?" Without warning, she abruptly exploded into an outburst, using obscene language, and said that I was always accusing her. Her accusation caught me by surprise because, before that, I had never even said a word to anyone inside that building. I was so angry, but kept my calm and quietly said, "Then, I'll just call the cops," and she shot back, "Call them. You go ahead and call them, and I'll tell them that you came upstairs and tried to force your way inside my apartment." She had an evil smirk on her face that caused me to look at her in disbelief. I instantly went mute, shook my head, closed the door behind me, and sprawled on the rug inside the living room, holding my head in pain. Once again, having faith in anyone was close to impossible and it made me realize how easily it is for innocent people to get themselves into trouble. Her behavior proved to me how dangerous she was and made me wonder how many people she had already accused.

The next morning after I got out of the shower, there was a loud thumping on the door, then I heard a female's voice yell, "He's in there, he's in there. He just doesn't want to answer." I looked through the peephole and saw her mother standing, puffing away like a giant, relating her daughter's fabricated story to a woman. "My daughter called me last night, screaming and crying on the phone, telling me that this child molester inside there came upstairs and tried to force his way inside my apartment." "What?! Are you sure about that?" asked the lady to whom the girl's mother was relating the story. "That's what my daughter said. She doesn't lie," the girl's mother replied. The lady replied, "It's hard for me to ever believe that he did that." The girl's mother burst out, "I don't trust him." I wanted to open the door to defend myself but was afraid that since I was only wearing a towel, appearing in front of them like that would have given them enough reason to believe the girl's story. I quickly slipped into my work clothes, then raced back to the door hoping to see them, but unfortunately, they had already left.

A few days later, I was in bed around 6 a.m. on a Saturday when suddenly I heard screaming along with a barrage of gunfire. I looked through the window and saw two young ladies tugging on the door of an apartment building that refused to budge as they continued to scream. Ten to fifteen feet away from them were two gunmen who were firing shots at them, but missed them both. The bullets ricochet off the steel door as shots rang out. How did two gunmen shoot from so close and missed both ladies? It had to be a miracle. All of a sudden, a patrol car that must have been parked in the area and heard the gunshots burst around the corner with tires screeching. One gunman instantly ceased fire and pretended as if he was casually walking down the sidewalk. The other gunman continued to fire and was still missing both women who were still tugging on the door. As the patrol car came to a stop, both officers raced out with guns drawn, and screamed "Freezeeeee, police. Drop the gun now." The gunman was reluctant at first, then hesitantly dropped the gun. While the officers disarmed him and placed him into handcuffs, one of the women suddenly shouted, "Look him dey! Look him dey!" as she pointed toward the other gunman who was casually walking down the sidewalk. The gunman took off, and one of the police officers jumped back inside the patrol car and chased after him.

Later that morning, I exited the building and closed the door behind me when out of nowhere, the mother of the girl who accused me of forcing my way inside her apartment barged into my face in a rage with a finger pointed at my eyes like a weapon. In fury, she burst out, "I heard you were trying to force your way inside my apartment to attack my daughter some night ago. Explicit, you lucky I wasn't at me." What?!, I replied before I quickly moved into the position of the security camera. With her finger still pointed just inches away from my eyes, she screamed, "You mother this and mother that try to force your way in." "Me?", I asked "Yes, you. Don't pretend that you're innocent now. I'll beat your (expletive) behind," she continued in her rage. "Take your hand out of my face," I said in a quiet but intimidating tone. "Move it, you faggot. Who the (expletive) do you think you are, threatening my daughter, and trying to force your way in? You (expletive) faggot-looking boy, trying to rape my daughter? Do you know who I am?" She continued to rant. My blood rushed to my head as my heart pounded. As much as I have never laid a hand on a female, I wanted to punch her in the face, then stamp her inside of her chest with a karate kick, then when she fell, beat my anger out of her, but instead, shook my head. Out of nowhere, a migraine came on, and my head began to pound worse than I'd ever felt it. I instantly became dizzy, felt like I wanted to faint, and staggered backward into a corner with my head resting on the door. She thought that I was scared and barged forward closer to my face, bust out louder, and began pounding on the door behind me. My head rattled. Out of the blue, her female counterpart limped from across the street on a cane, and began to scream from the top of her lungs, "Give it to him, give it to him. Kick his behind. What happened? You can't talk now? You had mouths that night when you tried to force your way inside her apartment to molest her daughter, but now you're quiet?" As everything went on, I stood my ground in shock as I looked at them, and thought how foolish they both were to believe everything a person says without any investigation or evidence. Slowly, a small crowd gathered, then my accuser popped out from hiding, "Oh, you don't have any mouth now, but you came to grab me the other night." I shot back, "You blatant liar," with my eyes locked onto her as my brain pounded against my skull. The mother then moved her fingers closer to my mouth, and I stared at her furiously, silently daring her to move it just a little closer to my lips so I could have bitten it off completely by a tooth that the dentist had already filed in preparation for a cap. Just then, someone opened the door behind me and I used the opportunity to re-enter the building and dial 911.

A crowd was still present when a male and female police officer pulled up in a patrol car. I raced downstairs and saw that before the police officer could exit their car, the girls' mother was already relating her hear-say side of the false story in a very polite manner to them. "I'm the one who called," I said, then both officers blew her off, exited the vehicle, and walked toward me. I used the opportunity to ask my accuser, "Excuse me, what did I say to you that night?" It was as if she couldn't understand the words that I was saying. She looked toward her mother for an answer. "Talk to me. Not her, " said the mother, and I sighed while looking at her, shaking my head. "Foolish. She's gonna get you in trouble," I said, but she never replied. The male officer took her and her daughter to one side as the female officer took me to the other side and then asked, "What happened?" "Well, all I did was ask her daughter to turn the music down the other night while she was coming down the stairway, and she burst out on me and then told her mother that I was trying to force my way inside her apartment. The mother saw me a few minutes ago and attacked me without asking any questions." "Did she touch you?" the officer asked. "No she didn't, but it was an attack," I said. "Did you try to force your way inside her apartment that night?" "No, I didn't even leave my apartment that night. All I did was crack the door slightly open, stuck my head out, and asked her to turn her music down." The questioning lasted about five minutes, then the policeman approached, followed by the girl and her mother as the mother continued, "He tried to attack my daughter." The policeman shot back, "There's no proof of him doing that." As the girl and her mother walked away, the policewoman turned to the policeman and said, "To be honest, I don't think he did anything," Upon hearing that, I assumed that based on the behavior of the three accusers, both officers realized that they were nothing but troublemakers.

Their misbehavior continued not too long after, when one day, seated at my computer, the toilet made a gulping sound, which caused me to quickly stop what I was doing and listen intently. There was silence, except for the low humming sound of my computer. Thinking that it was probably my imagination, I continued on my computer. Within seconds, there was a second gulp. I checked the bathroom to see what was happening. All of a sudden, water mixed with urine and feces burst out of the toilet bowl and splashed onto the bathroom floor with a disgusting smell. Like the flash character,

I bolted out of the bathroom and slammed the door shut behind me, and wasted no time in calling the building superintendent. There wasn't any answer. Not thinking straight, I called the fire department, assuming that with all their equipment, they'd assist me in clearing the blockage. They informed me that it wasn't a part of their job description, which I understood but was disappointed. There I was, restlessly pacing my living room floor as water gushed out the toilet bowl from time to time in an eight-story apartment building with approximately 32 units. After finally getting a hold of the superintendent who was some distance away, he arrived within an hour and a half. He cleared the blockage, cleaned and disinfected the bathroom, but stepping back inside it was quite sickening. Fifteen minutes later, the toilet continued to overflow. I called the superintendent again and he arrived in no time, then did the most disgusting thing I had ever seen. He placed his ungloved hand inside the toilet bowl, through feces and urine, and began to feel for whatever object was causing the blockage. As much as I wanted it cleared, I thought to myself, "How sickening," before I removed myself from the doorway. After nothing could be done, he closed the bathroom door and left. As the smell of feces and urine fetid the apartment, I left right behind him, then found myself relaxing inside the lobby for almost the entire day without even taking a shower or using the bathroom on that cold autumn Sunday. Later that night, a plumbing company came and cleared the blockage from the basement up to my apartment. They discovered that several sanitary pads were purposely flushed down the toilet by the girl and her mother, knowing that I was directly beneath them. They had an idea of the layout of the plumbing from a previous superintendent of the building who was a friend of the mother. The incident left me so disturbed that I placed several extra mats on the floor of the bathroom to prevent myself from stepping on the bare floor. Soon after, a memorandum was sent out to the entire building that warned everyone not to repeat any such behavior, which probably prompted the girl's mother to report me to the building management on several occasions. She stated that I was a troublemaker who wasn't supposed to be living inside the building. There were times when I was entering the building and she and her daughter shut the door in my face, but I said nothing about it. Even though I wasn't afraid of anyone and knew that I could have gotten back at the building management, to me, it was just best for me to leave.

CHAPTER TWELVE: WELCOME HOME

THE IDEA OF ME WANTING TO REFLECT ON WHERE EVERYTHING all started made me consider a much-needed break back to St. Vincent and the Grenadines. The Southern Grenadines, a chain of 31 islands, surrounded by white powdery sand and turquoise, transparent waters such as Mopiom, a sandy beach in the middle of the ocean nestled on a reef, and Tobago Cays being a diver's paradise where many eager the opportunity to swim with turtles like never before. Mystique, the most famous of them all, is mainly populated by some of the most famous people in the world. From Tommy Hilfiger, Brian Adams, Mick Jagger, and the late David Bowie. 15 miles North of it is mainland St. Vincent, the largest of them all. Its lush, expansive, magnificent landscape, breathtaking views and a volcano that I call "the Grand Canyon of the Caribbean '' is any hiker's dream who dares to take the challenge at 4000 feet.

The annual carnival festival, which begins in June and ends in July, was approaching. Considering that most of my friends home and abroad take their vacations during that time, meant that it was the best time for me to visit. The night before my trip, I was so afraid of missing my flight that I deprived myself of sleep. The following morning after I grabbed my suitcase, my mind was everywhere. It was as if I was in a daze and couldn't concentrate. At the time, there were no direct flights from New York to St. Vincent and the Grenadines. I had a connecting flight through a certain Caribbean island where I had to spend a few hours before I continued to St. Vincent on a smaller aircraft. Disoriented, tired and absent-minded, I pulled a stack of $500 U.S. out of an envelope from somewhere on my body that I can't remember up to this day. The cash was given to me by someone to hand over to a relative of theirs, in order to avoid a Western Union fee. I walked over to a young man seated on a bench to ask him a question. Before I could say a word, he pointed me toward a man standing not too far away whose eyes were locked onto me as if I was his target. Still not thinking straight, I approached the man, who immediately struck up a conversation with me as if we had known each other from birth. For some reason, I was dumb enough to feel at ease. He assisted me with my two suitcases over to an agent at the check-in counter and placed them onto the scale. Each suitcase was overweight by a certain amount which scared the crap out of me. "Oh man,! Now I have to pay for being overweight," I said, but to my surprise, the man told the agent not to charge me anything, and the agent said that it was ok. Up to that point, I still thought nothing of it until the aircraft took off. I started to search my entire body and my bag, then realized that the cash was gone. A couple of days into the Carnival festival, I got the shock of my life when the man walked towards me with a smile. "What are the chances of this even happening?" I asked myself as he approached me before bursting into a laugh as if nothing ever happened. As much as I wanted to confront him, I just couldn't. "What if it wasn't him?" I asked myself. On the other hand, the way his eyes were locked onto me as if I was his target, struck up a conversation as if he knew me all my life, assisted me with two suitcases, and made sure that I didn't have to pay for overweight caused me to think. Then again, there are still a small number of people who are filled with generosity, and he could very well be one of those people. The fact remained that I was disoriented and had no evidence of him taking the money. I could have very well been the one who misplaced it.

Costumes were on display everywhere as mass camps prepared for the festival. Soca and calypso music were blasting over numerous speakers, including at various picnics where I attended. I needed something more adventurous after just escaping the gray, gloomy years of some brutal winters that had me in solitary confinement for a duration of time. Like a group of poachers in search of a wild animal, a few of us journeyed to find hidden waterfalls where the only access was by foot. We found ourselves crossing streams through rocky areas deep inside rural, bushy, isolated areas. My adventure was cut short, however, after I was too afraid of visiting a waterfall called "Falls of Baleine". Its only access was by boat, and I wasn't willing to take that chance. Being from the Caribbean still doesn't make me fearless of the ocean in any way. Something about it scares the life out of me ever since I was a child, even though I lived about 200 meters from the sea. The idea of floating on water in the middle of nowhere surrounded by fish and mammals 20 times the size of man doesn't sit right with me.

Trips were made to three more places, one of them being Jamaica, Ocho Rios, my favorite place to be in Jamaica. Jamaica's landscape and winding roads in rural areas remind me so much of St. Vincent. The 11 visits that I made there convinced me that it was one of the islands where I can live, apart from St. Vincent and the Grenadines.

After a few days, I was back in New York City and had just finished grocery shopping when one of the people who encouraged me to return home shouted at me from across the street, "Hey, yow! What's up, man?" he shouted with excitement before he joined me on the sidewalk. After bumping fists, he continued, "So what's going on?" "Good" I answered as we chatted for a moment. "Everything ok?" he asked. As much as I wanted to say "No," my sixth sense told me that he was up to something, so I decided to tell him "Yes," to see how far he was willing to go. "I just got back from St. Vincent." His eyebrows raised, then he bobbed his head for a moment before he veered the conversation into what I had already expected. "Listen, I know you're living alone and everything, but I have this perfect girl for you," he said. Suspecting that he was talking about a relative of his who someone had already spoken to me about, I said nothing and decided to play along to see how far he was willing to go. "How long have you known this girl?" I asked, and he replied, "All my life because she's my cousin." he said. "As long as she's under 6' 1" because I'm not into any woman taller than I am," I said, and he burst out laughing. "Nah, man," he said, assuring me she was 5' 3" tall. "Ok," I said. Within a few days, the girl and I started chatting by phone almost every night, several nights a week, then a few days later met in person. Although she was very pretty, intelligent, very clean, and tidy–which is something I admire about a female–it didn't take long for me to figure out how sneaky she was and how much of a con artist. From the moment she entered my apartment, she confiscated my cordless phone for the entire day, and all of her calls were made and received from inside the bathroom. To hide the calls she made, she'd call random numbers of unknown people to try her best to deceive me. She was very much unaware that every call made and received was printed on my monthly bill. Almost everything that she said was made-up stories, which I realized due to her inconsistency. Whenever she asked anyone for help, she used the manipulative tactic of crying or pleading with that person while doing her best to convince them that they were the only ones she could have depended on. I was already aware of her motives, saw right through her and allowed her to slowly hang herself, then broke it off completely. Everything about her turned me off, and we still haven't spoken in years. I'm the type of person who will do my best to assist a person in any way possible, but if I tell you that I can't do something, don't try to use me because you'll turn me off. The moment I ever find out that you're trying to use me in any way, I'll have nothing to do with you for the rest of my life. Believe me, I'm an expert in casting people aside permanently and have absolutely no regrets about it.

It didn't take long for her cousin to find out that I got rid of her and like a counselor, he began his questioning. "What happened between the two of you, man?" he asked. "It just didn't work out, and let's just leave it alone," I said. He continued. "Man, that's a good girl for you, I'm telling you, dread." I responded, "Once again, it didn't work out, it is not going to work out, and I don't want it to work out." He went silent for a moment then after a sigh continued. "Listen, just stick with the girl for me please, nah man. You know how women have their ways." My mind was already made up. I was completely turned off by her behavior, but I knew exactly what he was getting at and wanted him to go into details so I said, "I'm not working for a lot of money, so I wouldn't be able to assist her in any way." He busted out, "No! No! No! That's not what I mean." I asked, "Then, what do you mean?" He responded, "I just want you to help her get herself organized." Still not being satisfied with his response, I wanted him to be more specific, so I replied, "You mean that she's looking for a place to stay? Because I don't understand what you mean." He paused for a moment, took a deep breath, released, then in a soft tone said, "Nah, man. I'm just asking if you can marry her to help her." With my head shaking, I smiled to myself, knowing that he was one of the people who encouraged me to return home when I was faced with my ordeal. As much as I was tempted to remind him about everything that he said, I thought of how childish it would be. Instead, I replied, "I don't love her, so I can't marry her." He paused for a moment, then said, "So you're saying that there's no way this can happen?" I replied, "No. Once my mind is made up on something, that's it!" He paused for a moment then said. "So, you can't help a sister out?" I replied, "The sister is going about doing things the wrong way, and I'm not going to ever get caught up in this illegal crap. I'm sure she'll find someone who she honestly loves, and who honestly loves her." With that, I ended the conversation and went my separate way. Everything about him and the attitude of his cousin showed me how much people enjoy taking advantage of others, and the distance they're

217

willing to go to do it, especially once they see that you're quiet. The truth is that quiet and generous people could very well be nasty, we just choose not to be.

CHAPTER THIRTEEN:
FAREWELL

The morning was freezing and as I got out of bed, an unexplainable, psychogenic pain came over me as I walked toward the window, confused as to whether a migraine was triggered for unknown reasons or whether I was somehow overtaken by the sudden effect of food poisoning from a cookout the previous day. The more I thought about it, there wasn't any abdominal pain, upset stomach, or nausea, which are all associated with food poisoning. As a form of precaution, I decided to remain at home and called one of my friends who was a Nurse, but there wasn't any answer.

Out of nowhere, the image of my mother twirled through my head like a windmill, and a restless feeling came over me that caused me to pace the floor back and forth with my arms folded in confusion left me to wonder if I was experiencing anxiety or ataraxy. After turning the television on in the hope that it would clear my mind, I sprawled onto the couch. Within two minutes, the phone rang. Convinced that it was my nurse friend, I quickly answered, laughing, then said, "You're an angel, do you know that?" with the expectation of hearing her reply, "Thank you very much, sir" followed by her usual giggle. Instead, it was the soft, quiet, sympathetic tone of my aunt on the other end of the phone who said, "Your mother just died." I froze for a minute as I tried to figure out if I heard correctly, but couldn't utter another word. I released a sigh and lowered my head to the floor in silent anguish. My blood gushed from my feet up to my head. A mild, bearable headache came on out of nowhere and to prevent a migraine, I released a second sigh, then quietly shook my head. "Sorry for everything you went through," she continued, but at that moment, I couldn't take it anymore. I said, "Thank you," and then ended the call.

    I laid back on the couch with both palms of my hands behind the back of my head as I stared vacantly at the ceiling. In a silent state of oblivion where absolutely nothing mattered anymore and hope completely disappeared, I closed my eyes, and all of my childhood memories of her flashed across my mind. Her funny laughs, her smiles, and how she took care of my sister and me. My eyes became watery and as the tears streamed from the side of my face, I reopened my eyes and stared at the ceiling, expecting God's face to appear so I could ask Him, " Why did he take her away from us so soon after not seeing her for almost 14 years?" Then I remembered that during the years that she was missing, I had asked Him to please allow my sister and me to be with her one final time. I could only assume that after he had fulfilled his bargain, it was His turn to take her back. It struck me like a brick after not realizing that the conversation I had with her the previous day was our last conversation. She sounded healthy. Nothing indicated to me that she was ill unless she was and no one told me. To get the call one day after that she was dead puzzled me.

I pondered constantly how to break the news to my younger sister, who was no longer four years old but spoke with her by phone periodically. Their unconditional love for each other was quite indescribable. It was quite evident from the moment I stepped inside the house. Their bond was unbreakable, how she hugged our mother, respected her, recognized her incapabilities, and was always at her side ready and willing to assist her in every way without hesitation. To see her comfort me during my broken times during my visit, was unbelievable for a four-year-old, something that I couldn't do at that age. The more I thought about it, I wished that there was a recognizable award of achievement to be presented to her, but I believe that God has His way of blessing her.

With my arms folded, I glanced at the clock for a second time, then released a quiet sigh, shook my head, then slipped into a jacket, and exited the apartment before I stepped into the brutal cold. Calmly wandered through the street with both hands tucked inside my jacket pocket as I moved past everyone with my head tilted to the ground as though they were all invisible. Those who greeted me with a simple "Good morning," went on deaf ears. Being in the open was where I always wanted to be because it helped me to forget about everything, but the smooth-flowing traffic that once calmed my mind sounded like a race car track. The cold month of November transformed every beautiful, fertile spring tree into brown and unbearable trees that appeared like a vast of timber, rooted to the ground. Everything brought back the memories of my mother dragging toward me with her trembling hands as tears streamed down her cheeks. It played out in my head like a mantra. Fortunately, it was only a figment of my imagination.

    After returning home, I quietly sat on the couch for almost an hour, staring into space, pondering the decision once again of calling my sister. After a moment of sighing, I hesitantly reached for the phone with my trembling hand, took one final breath before a vacant stare, then dialed the number. The phone rang for a moment before her father answered and to avoid a long conversation, off the bat, I said "Good morning, please tell my sister that our mom just passed." "Oh, man, I'll tell her," he said. Not for once did he offer any form of condolence or asked how she died. Instead, he babbled on about things that didn't interest me. My blood began to boil and I felt a migraine coming on and asked, "May I please speak with my sister?" He handed her the phone without saying another word. "Hi," she said in her sweet, Southern accent, which brought a teardrop to my eyes. It was hard for me to begin as I stood there for a quiet moment, about to break the news to a child under the age of 10 that her mother who she loved and cared for and missed more than anything else, was dead. Though I'm not a psychologist or have any form of degree in the medical field, it didn't take much for me to realize the effect it would have had on her. I wanted to break the news as slowly and as carefully as I possibly could. After a pause, I took one deep final breath, and with my eyes closed, I exhaled and said, "Mummy's dead." The phone became so silent that there wasn't even the sound of a sidetone. I thought that I had lost connection and said, "Hello?" a few times before she responded, "Yeah" in a low tone beneath her breath. I sighed, shook my head in anguish, and tried my best to console her. All of her answers were quiet, delayed responses of "Hmmm," which indicated sadness and reminded me of the times my mom spent on the phone replying "Yes" and "No." I was at a loss for words, and once again there was silence before her father returned to the line and said, "She needs to go now," and I replied "No problem," then the phone went dead.

The following morning was cold and gray, and as much as I tried to remain at home, the brutally, gloomy weather brought nothing but sad memories. I decided that it was best to head to work, where the news had already reached a few of my coworkers who were in shock to see me appear at the workplace. "Boy, what are you doing here? You're supposed to be home today. Your mother died," one coworker said. The supervisor overheard, then called me aside. "What happened?" he asked, and after I informed him of my mother's death, he said, "Take a couple of days off," without even asking if I wanted to. I pleaded with him to let me remain at work so that I could have kept my mind occupied, but the more I pleaded, the more he insisted that I leave. Little did anyone know that home was where all the memories lived. "Come back the following Monday," he said, then I shook my head, sighed, and without saying another word, slipped into my jacket and quietly left. I found myself on a bench at Union Square Park, completely spaced out all alone. My only company was the thousands of dried, colored, fallen leaves discarded amongst snirt. I wasn't even bothered by the buffs of arctic wind that rattled hundreds of twigs hung from the brown and barren trees on that brutally cold November morning. The more I thought of my sister, a smile appeared on my face. Instead of crying, I was suddenly awakened from my daydream as the cold penetrated my shoes and body. To defrost myself, I stepped inside a nearby Barnes and Noble where I spent countless hours seated on the floor with a book in hand with not even the slightest craving for a bite of anything.

CHAPTER FOURTEEN:
KARMA AND THE CONCLUSION

After getting in touch with an independent movie director who taught me the fundamentals of screenwriting, I went into studying the craft. Weekend after weekend, I shot independent movies alongside independent directors who taught me everything they knew. My mind was bombarded with memories of the prior years and putting the first draft of this book together tortured me constantly with flashbacks each time I attempted to write. After the pandemic placed me under house arrest, I reflected on everything more and my years of procrastination expired. I had no choice but to face my fear and disclose everything to the world.

There are still times when I sit back and shake my head, wondering "What could have been" if I'd never attempted to see my mother again. Although it wasn't something that anyone ever expected me to do, it just wasn't something that I was ever willing to let slip by.

As time elapsed and the internet began to boom, my curiosity about the people I encountered during my ordeal crossed my mind. As for my mother's ex-husband, I can only wish that he would take the time to reflect on his evil deeds and ask God for forgiveness, but with a narcissist, that's pretty much impossible since they can never see the wrong or hurt that they cause to anyone. To them, accepting responsibility and apologizing are signs of weakness and defeat, something a narcissist isn't willing to accept. The fact that my sister was only four years old at the time and may have only heard one side of the story, makes it only fair to assume she has unanswered questions. She deserves to hear the truth, and even though there is so much more that I can say, for now, I'll refrain.

Many may consider me to take things lightly, but exposing those who do me wrong is never a part of my agenda. The truth has a way of revealing itself no matter how long it takes, and the evil that we do to each other has a way of catching up with us. That was quite evident with my former friend and his girlfriend who left me bankrupt, then turned their backs on me. The only information I had concerning them was that they had lost their apartment for obvious reasons and were living separate ways. From my experience, I had no doubt that they were somewhere scouting another victim while using their innocent child who was no longer a baby as a way of gaining compassion. As much as I felt pity toward the innocent child, I wasn't going to be burnt a second time.

I was very determined to find out whatever happened to the girl I met on that Caribbean island. On a hunch, I decided to search Facebook. There she was in a photograph with her daughter, both were looking much more mature and were posing with beautiful impeccable smiles with dimples on both sides of their cheeks. Nothing about her features had changed, but to know that she was living in New York with her mother almost made me shed a tear. Instead, I smiled. After days of chatting by phone, we finally met up. She admitted that she was searching for me as well on Facebook, but I was pretty much hard to find since I was using the name of a character borrowed from a movie sequel with the phrase, "My name's B......... J B." For an entire summer up to the winter, we hung out, but the more time I spent with her, I came to realize that many are not who they appear to be and that some people only cross your path for a reason. Whether or not my reason for meeting her was to help her reconcile her differences with her mother, I'll never know. The season came, ended very quickly and I said to myself, "So be it," and moved on to a new direction.

As for the attorney who swindled me out of every dime, the truth about him was much easier than ever to find due to the dominance of Google. A simple search of him revealed everything that my instinct was warning me about from the first time I stepped inside his office but was foolish enough to continue. According to the stories found in an article that I still have as a souvenir, he neglected some of his clients who then reported him and caused him to be disbarred. I thought about how much I should have done the same thing after paying him all of my hard-earned money for a case he purposely never completed. Instead, I shook my head and figured he'd have his day. As I continued to read the article, it stated that he was nabbed at a New York courthouse after he attempted to defend someone even after he was disbarred. To me, it shows that he was so accustomed to the habit of misleading many that it became such an obsession, he thought that he was very much above the law. I still believe that his porch office was nothing more than a sham to deceive the innocent who hired him for a service he knew he might not even complete. As many say, life is a cycle and whatever a person gives out, comes back to them. If there's such a thing as karma, then it has a vicious way of repaying those who treat us unfairly.

ABOUT THE AUTHOR

Rodney Pemberton is a screenwriter, an underground singer/songwriter, and now an author from the Caribbean Island of St. Vincent and the Grenadines. Both his father and grandfather were skilled pianists, but Rodney's passion for music lies in singing and writing. He decided to study the craft of screenwriting after migrating to New York City. In 2022, he released "Rendezvous Reboot," which reached No.40 on the UK Itunes charts, and "Waters," which was produced by Billboard's Top Ten artists, and Grammy U, mento Oliver Sean. It went straight to No. 1 on the UK Itunes charts. More information on Rodney can be found on both his website and Instagram pages: More about him can be found below on his website and Instagram page.

https://www.imanient.com
https://www.instagram.com/rodpemberton/